風水
FENG SHUI
FOR YOU AND YOUR
CAT

Watson-Guptill Publications
NEW YORK

Copyright © 2000 THE IVY PRESS LIMITED   First published in 2000 in the United States of America by Watson-Guptill Publications, a division of BPI Communications, Inc., 1515 Broadway, New York, NY 10036.

All rights reserved. No part of this book may be reproduced or used in any form or by any means—graphic, electronic, or mechanical, including photocopying, recording, taping, or information storage and retrieval systems—without written permission of the publisher.

Library of Congress Catalog Card Number: 99-66040 ISBN 0-8230-1655-2

This book was conceived, designed, and produced by THE IVY PRESS LIMITED, The Old Candlemakers, West Street, Lewes, East Sussex, England BN7 2NZ

Art Director: PETER BRIDGEWATER   Editorial Director: DENNY HEMMING   Managing Editor: ANNE TOWNLEY   Designer: GLYN BRIDGEWATER   Senior Project Editor: ROWAN DAVIES

Copy Editors: RONNE RANDALL AND HILARY WESTON   Prop Hunter: FRANKIE GOLDSTONE   Photography: GUY RYECART   Picture Researcher: LIZ EDDISON

Illustrations: LORRAINE HARRISON, CATHERINE MCINTYRE, ANDREW KULMAN, SARAH YOUNG

Printed and bound in China by Sun Fung Offset Binding Company Limited. 1 2 3 4 5 6 7 8 9 10/ 09 08 07 06 05 04 03 02 01 00

This book is typeset in 9.5/14 Gill Sans Light.

contents

introduction

Looking at your cat curled up asleep in her favorite spot, you might find it hard to believe that while she appears to be peacefully snoozing, she's actually working hard on your behalf! Obviously, you take good care of your cat; you feed her, keep her warm and watch her health, but you probably don't expect much in return except a purr of contentment. However, the truth is that your cat is a veritable powerhouse of energy that can help to enhance your own well-being and even improve your prosperity.

As the pace of life becomes more hectic, people are looking to ancient wisdom to find ways to create peace and contentment in their lives. Consequently, feng shui (pronounced "fung shway")—which literally means "wind and water"—has become popular in recent years.

RIGHT **Curled up in repose, yet with eyes and ears constantly monitoring the world, your cat is a perfect example of the yin-yang principle at work, opposite energies working together in harmony.**

There are a number of schools of feng shui, but the two most widespread ones are known as the Form School and the Compass School, and these are the ones we shall draw on in this book. Their basic principles are easy for the beginner to grasp, but feng shui is a fascinating subject and you may well find that you want to learn more about it and ways in which you can refine it. In that case, we would recommend you seek out some of the excellent books listed in the Further Reading section (see p. 157).

LEFT Your cat's very presence in your home encourages "good vibes" in the form of sheng chi.

In its most basic form, feng shui involves employing a few simple rules to banish or moderate energy which is either too sluggish (si chi) or fast-moving (sha chi)—both being equally harmful to the occupants of your home—and free up healthy energy (sheng chi), encouraging it to flow and spread its beneficial effects around your house.

YOUR CAT AS A FENG SHUI EXPERT

As a cat lover, you will know how much positive emotion is generated by your pet. Amazingly enough, that "warm glow" of affection you both feel when she is curled up on your lap when you are sitting in a cozy armchair is a very real force of energy. Her presence alone within your home will assist you in ways that you may never have dreamed of.

Aside from the loving warmth she spreads throughout your home, your cat can help you to implement good feng shui practices in so many different ways. By observing the places where she likes to sit around the house, you can identify the areas of your life, such as work, relationships, and family, that need working on and, with her help, can put into action measures that will improve the quality of your life. She can also show

BELOW **If your cat chooses to settle in an unusual place, she may have discovered an area of stale chi or geopathic stress.**

you the places within your home where it is unwise to spend too much time, either sitting, studying, or sleeping —the areas where unhealthy energy accumulates or where geopathic stress leaks into your house, which could prove harmful if you expose yourself to it for long periods—and help to neutralize these negative conditions.

WORKING WITH YOUR CAT

Your relationship, however, is not a one-way street. By being sensitive to your cat's needs, you can improve her quality of life as well. As you acquire knowledge about the principles of feng shui, you can help her to balance the home environment, thus protecting her from either being overworked in transmuting negative energy or overloaded by positive energy. Once you've struck the right balance, you will both be happier and at peace with your surroundings and able to enjoy life to the fullest.

Don't forget that feng shui isn't limited to the inside of your home. The ancient Chinese were also well-versed in constructing gardens that were both beautiful and practical, and a well-planned garden can function as an additional boost to the remedies that you introduce within your home, helping to alleviate negative forces. In addition, it has the bonus of being an attractive and welcoming place where both you and your cat can relax and recharge your energies. With a helpful cat in your house, there is no need to hire a feng shui expert. Your cat is a natural practitioner of feng shui, so use her innate skills to make it work for you.

ABOVE Feng shui is rooted in the ancient landscape of China; its name means "wind and water," and it was originally developed as a method of working with the elemental energies, harnessing the power of the benign, and neutralizing the influence of the bad.

complementary
feng shui for you
and your cat

風水配
合你和
你的貓

the ancient, mysterious cat

Ever since they first came in from the Egyptian deserts and lived alongside human beings, cats have been credited with mysterious powers. Watch your cat as she sits regally in a window with her tail curled neatly around her, or as she stalks stiff-legged into the kitchen, loudly demanding her dinner, or as she arches her back and spits vehemently on being confronted with a threat. When you see this kind of behavior, it's easy to understand how the ancient Egyptians came to worship these enigmatic creatures as deities—and why, in the Middle Ages, Europeans came to fear them as the familiars of witches.

BELOW **A seemingly instinctive love of luxury reinforces the regal image that cats have enjoyed in many cultures since ancient times.**

TREASURED HELPERS

It wasn't their looks alone that persuaded the ancient Egyptians to place cats on a level with gods. Domesticated cats also served a practical purpose by catching the rodents that fed on precious stores of grain. To people living at subsistence level, their cats' efficiency as pest controllers could mean the difference between life and starvation.

Ancient Egyptian felines worked hard for their living—as well as protecting the food stores, they also killed poisonous snakes and were used for hunting wild fowl, as dogs are used today. In return, they were made the subject of such veneration that to steal or kill a cat became an offense punishable by death.

LEFT **Contemporary cats have lost none of the mystery that so fascinated the Egyptians; an enigmatic pose is second nature to them and it is easy to believe that they have privileged access to the secrets of the universe.**

RIGHT **A cat mummy from Egypt, dating from c. B.C. 1000–332. By the time of the pharaohs of the New Kingdom (c. B.C. 1530–663), the cat had been deified in the form of the goddess Bastet, and was worshipped at her temple at Bubastis.**

ORIENTAL HUNTERS

Early records of the existence of cats have also been discovered in China. Here too, they were treasured in their role as hunters. This was doubly important in China, for as well as guarding food supplies, they also protected the silkworms, essential for the valuable silk trade.

Strange though it may seem to modern-day Westerners, the Chinese did not make pets of their cats. Instead, they treated them as they would any other working agricultural animal, keeping them reined in on leashes—and in some regions, even fattening them up for food!

Those early felines may seem very far removed from the much-loved animal now dozing on your windowsill, but today's domestic cats are direct descendants of those Chinese and Egyptian hunters. If pressed, many would be able to fend for themselves in a semi-wild state.

cats in ancient China

In ancient China, as in Egypt, cats were credited with supernatural powers. However, whereas in Egypt they were usually associated with the more positive aspects of life, such as the sun and fertility, many of the superstitions that grew up around them in China took a darker turn.

RIGHT According to Chinese lore, cats of a certain color or pattern can be magnets for money and wealth.

GOOD OR EVIL?

Some cats were viewed favorably. In northern China, for example, the god who protected the harvest, Li-Shou, was depicted as a cat, but this cult did not spread to the rest of China. The Butterfly Cat, whose pelt had spots rather than stripes, was considered lucky, as were cats whose coat was a particular shade of gold, because they were thought to attract wealth.

In the main, though, the Chinese considered cats to have associations with the darker side of the occult. The Yellow Emperor did not include them in his list of the 12 animals that form the Chinese Zodiac. (One legend says that cats hunt down and kill rats in revenge for the fact that the Rat tricked the Cat out of his place in the Zodiac and took it himself.) Cats were also thought to be in league with demons.

SUPERSTITIONS AND TALISMANS

Like its bigger cousins, such as the tiger and the lion, the cat was believed to have the ability to chase away evil spirits. Anyone who has witnessed Chinese New Year celebrations will have seen the Lion Dances, which are intended not only to usher in good luck, but also to put bad influences and spirits to flight. The cat's abilities were reputed to be so powerful that merely putting a picture of a cat in a strategic place in the home was thought to be just as effective as having a living animal.

Nowadays, we give no more credence to these kinds of superstitions than we would do to the medieval belief that witches could transform themselves into cats during the course of their rituals. Nevertheless, at the end of the twentieth century, cats—like many other living creatures—are probably more in tune with the energies and tensions to be found in nature than most human beings are, and this is something that becomes especially obvious to those who practice feng shui. While you think your cat is quietly napping in a dark corner or on a remote shelf, she may be bringing her own, peculiarly beneficial influence to bear on your home and consequently, your life. It is important to be able to enhance this influence.

ABOVE Seemingly dozing, a pair of cats work together to counteract the poison arrow energy coming from the horizontal lines of the wooden stairs.

what is feng shui?

To start at the most basic level, the words "feng shui" mean "wind and water," and the purpose of feng shui is to enable you to live in greater harmony with your environment, i.e. the winds and waters of the earth. Creating this harmony will in turn have a beneficial effect on how your life progresses. Feng shui evolved out of the principles of Taoism and the concept of balance that lies at its heart. Feng shui practitioners believe that, by moderating the flow of the energies that surround you, you can bring order and harmony into your everyday life, and this is where your cat can help you. She is peculiarly sensitive to these energies and can also have a beneficial effect on them, as you will learn as you read on.

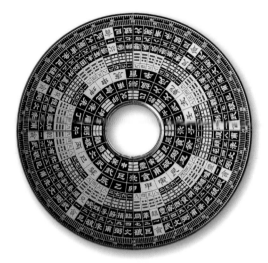

EARLY BEGINNINGS

The origins of feng shui go back more than 4,000 years, to the time when China's legendary first emperor, Fu Hsi, is said to have discovered the basis of the *I Ching*, or *Book of Changes*, an early work used in fortune-telling. Originally, knowledge and practice of feng shui were restricted to the Chinese upper classes, but over many hundreds of years its theory evolved and spread. It has continued to flourish in modern times, even though it was outlawed under Mao Zedong from 1949 to 1976.

MODERN APPLICATIONS

Feng shui is just as applicable today as it ever was, even though modern life is much further removed from nature and natural forces than in those far-off days, and is growing steadily more complex. In places such as Hong Kong and Singapore, few people would consider moving into a new home or building a new office without first consulting a feng shui expert to advise them on advantageous locations, hidden hazards, and the like.

And does it work? Well, let's put it this way. Many of the principles of feng shui—such as keeping rooms clean and free from clutter—are grounded in good old common sense.

Perhaps the best way of gathering evidence of feng shui's effectiveness is to visit a room before and after it has been arranged by a practitioner. After they have finished, a more soothing, nurturing, and supportive atmosphere becomes evident. Certainly, experimenting with the precepts of feng shui won't do you any harm—so you might as well try them and see if they will do you, and your cat, any good.

ABOVE **A Lo Pan pa kua** compass. Such an elaborate example would probably only be used by an expert.

LEFT **Peace, harmony, and freedom from clutter** are the ultimate goals of successful feng shui.

RIGHT **Hong Kong, a city** built following feng shui principles and one of the richest cities in the world.

yin, yang, and the importance of balance

To understand the concepts on which feng shui is based, it's essential to grasp the Taoist principles of yin and yang. These are the two polarities which are apparent throughout the natural world and which, when united, create tao. In English, tao translates as "the way," a concept which is hard to define, but roughly means the guiding force behind the course of the entire universe, including one's own life.

ABOVE **Earth and sky, female and male, night and day, water and wind, cat and dog; all yin and yang, respectively.**

RIGHT **Balance comes easily to cats, who can relax even when posed on a precariously small pedestal.**

▌ HEAVEN AND EARTH

In general, yin is concerned with all things earthly and yang with the ethereal. Everything that exists can be divided into one or other of these categories, as shown at right.

It's important for Westerners to understand that yang is not better than yin, or vice versa. The point is that they coexist; if you look at the ancient yin-yang symbol, you will see that each half contains a complementary circle of its opposite, illustrating that each contains an element of the other. What is most important is that they are in perfect harmony and balance.

It is this harmony and balance that we must seek to duplicate in our lives if we are to create the most favorable circumstances in which to live. To take an extreme example, no human could live at either of the icy poles because they are too yin for survival, while, equally, the deserts of the world are too yang.

ABOVE **The yin-yang symbol encapsulates the concept of energies in harmony. Enclosed in a circle, the dark yin and the bright yang embrace each other, each containing a seed of the other buried within itself.**

▌ DOMESTIC HARMONY

But as well as seeking a balance between yin and yang in the outside world, the two must also be in harmony within the home. For example, if you find yourself constantly on the go and wearing yourself out as you rush from one activity to another—a classic yang state—you may need to surround yourself with more yin energy to create a less stressful and more restful home environment. Put some "quiet time" aside every day to sit down in an armchair with your cat on your lap. As you stroke her back and listen to her soothing purr, put your goals and worries to one side for a few minutes and just enjoy being at peace with your cat. If, on the other hand, you feel bored and lethargic, you may need more yang energy around you to stir things up a bit. Get up off that sofa, get down on the floor, and play some games with your cat. Cats love to play, and even if you're only rolling a piece of screwed-up newspaper across the floor for her to chase, you're both having fun and creating some beneficial yang energy in the room at the same time.

Every individual is different, with varying needs and preferences as to the kind of life to lead. It is essential, therefore, that you are successful in finding the right balance, the one that makes you happy. And your cat can help you to explore what is missing in that all-important search for personal harmony.

five elements

Yin and yang—that is, all things in the natural world—can be broken down into what are known as the five elements. These elements comprise the universe's principal energies, which are fire, metal, water, wood, and earth. Conversely, these five elements are also contained within all things, including ourselves—and, of course, our cats! Chinese astrologers believe that they are also incorporated into our individual horoscopes. However, their properties are not rigidly fixed—the balance between them within each person or thing varies, and one element always predominates.

BELOW Water, fire, metal, wood, and earth are the five elements that should interact with each other to make a balanced whole.

THE NATURE OF THE ELEMENTS

Each element has its own set of characteristics; these will help you to understand feng shui.

FIRE Fire is associated with the color red. It is a very strong element and is concerned with excitement and enjoyment, but it must be treated with caution; if it is not, it can get out of control and become destructive. A fire person loves to be continually stimulated and cannot bear to be bored.

METAL Metal is associated with the colors silver, gold, and white. Because coins are made of metal, this element symbolizes financial wealth. However, knives and swords are also made of metal, so it can be a very aggressive element. Metal types tend to have controlling personalities and enjoy neatness and order.

WATER Water is associated with the colors black and blue and, like metal, symbolizes financial wealth. Water often represents renewal as well. Despite its fluid nature, it is a very potent element—too much water can result in an overwhelming flood, and water continually coursing over a surface will gradually wear away even the most resilient of rocks. Water types are sensitive, intelligent, and very good communicators.

WOOD As the symbol of growth, wood is associated with the colors green and brown. Because of its association with plants, wood is a very powerful symbol in feng shui. Plants can be used to soften sharp corners, stimulate wealth, or represent longevity—even artificial blooms can have their uses! Wood types are sociable, creative, and positive.

EARTH Earth is associated with the colors yellow and brown. Placed in the middle of the yin-yang symbol, it is also related to the center of the home and has a stabilizing effect. Earth is a strong and reliable element, but if overused, can exert an influence that is too stolid and dull. Earth types are diplomatic, loyal, and try to be helpful to others.

The five elements interact in two ways—the productive and destructive cycles. You will learn more about these later (*see pp. 82–83*), when we look at some ways in which you can experiment with increasing the harmony within your home.

FAR LEFT **Cats** are fascinated by water, at least at a distance. Water nourishes wood, which, in turn, is the element associated with cats.

the flow of chi

Yin and yang were created by chi, which is the electromagnetic energy force that flows throughout the universe. It circulates around the body of every living creature, from the tiniest insect to the biggest mammal. In human beings, it courses between the seven chakras (or "meridians"), which are located at the top of the head, between the eyes, the throat, the center of the chest, the solar plexus, just below the navel, and at the base of the spine. Each chakra is believed to govern different parts of the body and different areas of our lives.

ABOVE RIGHT **An artistic representation of the chi of cats. Chi is at once ever-flowing yet calm, a quality that cats also possess.**

FAR RIGHT **Chi flows in and out of your house through the front door. Your cat will often station herself on the open threshold, monitoring the energy flow.**

RIGHT **In all animals, including humans and cats, life energy is thought to flow through the power points in the body known as the chakras.**

IN, OUT, AND ALL AROUND

Chi doesn't just flow within us—it also flows throughout the things which make up our external surroundings. As it does so, it is affected by both the natural and the man-made features it encounters, just as water on its way toward the sea will become turbulent as it tumbles over rocks, calmed when its channel becomes broader, or polluted by a chemical spill or industrial waste. In much the same way, when chi passes by a hospital, it will be tainted by the pain and suffering it picks up there. When it streams through a beautiful natural landscape of gently undulating green hills, it becomes refreshed and revitalized. Similarly, its movement will be slowed when it comes up against a large, solid obstacle like a mountain or a skyscraper, calmed as it passes along the path of a curving stream or meandering country lane, and quickened when it is channeled along a fast-flowing river or a busy highway.

CATS AND CHI

Of course, chi swirls around outside our houses, and when we open doors and windows, we let it into our homes. One of the things it's going to encounter in your home is your cat—and the good news is that she brings a beneficial influence to bear on chi, for two main reasons. The first is that she is such a lively, inquisitive creature, always on the move, and consequently stirring up chi wherever she goes around the house. The second is the love and affection that she generates from you and the other occupants of your home and which she gives back in return, thus providing a source of good chi within your house. The chi within our home affects our well-being and health, our state of mind and emotions, and also our luck in life. It's when we achieve the perfect balance of chi—what the Chinese call sheng chi, or "the cosmic breath of the dragon"—that our lives will begin to flourish at their optimum level.

negative chi

Ideally, chi should flow around a home freely and smoothly, preferably along the line of curves, and at moderate speed. This is healthy chi, which will facilitate good luck for the house's occupants. But when the chi surrounding and within our homes is out of balance, it cannot bring benefits to us, and we may begin to run into problems. What feng shui practitioners seek to avoid at all costs is si chi and sha chi.

SI CHI

Stagnant chi (si chi) is weak and sluggish, slowed down by encountering too many obstacles and sullied by dirt, stale air, and bad smells. Chi can also be made stale and stagnant by becoming trapped in corners and blind alleys, from which it cannot find an exit, or by being entangled in household clutter. When si chi moves slowly around a house, it can make the occupants feel lethargic and constantly tired, and may prove a drain on their resources.

SHA CHI

More dangerous, though, is sha chi, the "killing breath." This is chi which is either running too fast, because it is channeled along a straight line with no obstacles in its path, or is concentrated into a specific point, to form a potentially hazardous "poison arrow." When sha chi is rushing past or through a building at speed, it prevents its occupants from living in peace by causing aggression and conflict, while poison arrows slice through auspicious influences and may destroy them altogether.

Within the home, fast-running sha chi may be caused by features like long, unbroken, straight corridors; areas of concentrated sha chi may be caused by sharp corners that protrude into rooms, like pillars or cupboards.

IMPROVING CHI

Have you ever noticed how one store in a shopping area never appears to prosper, while all the others do well? Or have you observed how a particular house in a street always seems to look run-down, and that its hapless inhabitants are constantly getting behind with rent or mortgage payments, or are suffering marital, family, or health problems? Feng shui consultants will claim that this is due to accumulated sha chi, and much of their work is concerned with seeking it out, both inside and outside the house, and countering, or at least neutralizing, its influence. You have an extra ally in defeating si and sha chi in your cat, who can help you to convert it into more positive energy by bringing her beneficial influence to bear within the home environment.

ABOVE Too many objects can obstruct the flow of chi. If your cat is prowling around a cluttered area of the home, it may be time to rearrange your belongings.

LEFT Spiral staircases are considered inauspicious because they suck chi into a vortex which runs through the house.

FAR LEFT A cat on a hot tin roof. The cat is working both for herself (it's a warm spot for a nap) and to prevent the precipitate rush of energy down the straight channels of the corrugated roofing.

countering negative chi

If you live in a sleepy cul-de-sac, you may feel pleased that you are providing a safe environment for your cat. As we all know, it's impossible to teach a cat road sense. They simply believe—quite rightly!—that all traffic should give way to them and squeal to a halt the minute they set a paw on the road. Sadly, this often isn't the case. Nevertheless, although a quiet road may help your cat to live longer, it can also lead to si chi. Or perhaps you have the opposite problem, and need to counter sha chi because you live on a very busy road. Or maybe your home is the focal point of a "poison arrow" due to the positioning of a neighboring building or a roofline pointing at the front of your house. Perhaps you live at a junction where chi energy is concentrated on your front door.

ABOVE If your cat seems to spend a lot of her time sitting in the same spot outside the front of your house, it may be time to look at the orientation of your entrance door and consider relocating it.

NEGATIVE CHI SITUATIONS

This house faces the "poison arrow" of a T-junction. The full force of sha chi hits the front door head on.

A house in a cul de sac may be afflicted by si chi which gathers and stagnates in what is literally a "dead end."

A house situated on a busy road may be subject to dangerous levels of sha chi caused by the flow of traffic past the front door.

ABOVE The position of your house in relation to roads, other buildings, or natural features influences the kind of chi that flows your way. These three positions are considered inauspicious.

RIGHT Watch your cat as she patrols the house; it will help you to pinpoint the places where negative chi gathers in your home.

CREATING BARRIERS

The best way to deal with all of these situations is to create a barrier, in the form of a fence or a hedge, between your home and the sha chi. The barrier doesn't have to be very high—its symbolism as a defense is more important than its role as a physical obstacle. When more drastic action is called for, bear in mind that your front door's relationship to its surroundings is most important. Moving the front door or constructing a porch can help by relocating the entrance to a more auspicious position, but you may find it easier to simply use another entrance to the home.

PA KUA MIRRORS

As a last resort, you might consider hanging a pa kua mirror outside your front door. This is an octagonal mirror that can deflect poison arrows—which is why it should only ever be used out of doors, and never inside the home. Be careful that none of your neighbors' houses are captured in its reflection, as it will divert the poison arrow toward them. If you decide to use a pa kua mirror, make sure you get the help and advice of a professional feng shui practitioner. The pa kua mirror is a very powerful feng shui tool, and its use in unskilled hands may cause more harm than good.

your sensitive cat

As any cat lover knows, most cats will spend many contented hours sitting at a front window, quietly watching the traffic go by, almost as if they're hypnotized by its movement. Why? When they're out of doors, they tend to ignore traffic and certainly never adopt the futile and uncouth canine practice of chasing cars and cyclists. Could it be that as they watch the movement from the window, they are drawing on the chi generated by the passing vehicles?

▌ A MODEL OF POISE AND BALANCE

The fact is that cats are just as sensitive to chi as human beings are—in fact, they're more sensitive. Just look at your cat, and you'll see that she is the perfect embodiment of the kind of poise and balance that feng shui sets out to achieve. Everything about a cat's being and behavior seems to be a model of grace and equilibrium: the delicate curve of her arched back; the way her tail curls almost into a question mark when she is inquisitive; the smooth and elegant arc her body describes as she leaps from one vantage point to another; the soothing purr she makes when she is content; the fastidious manner in which she keeps herself clean and dry; the way she tucks herself into a neat ball when she sleeps—in fact, the yin-yang symbol could almost be an abstract picture of two cats entwined around each other!

▌ WILD CATS

While humans have evolved and become more "sophisticated," distancing themselves from nature with technological wonders like cars, televisions, and telephones, your cat is still in touch with the primeval instincts of her wilder ancestors, who relied upon them to survive. So while you may have the feeling that something is "not quite right" in your home, your cat can pinpoint exactly where the unhealthy energies are—and what's more, she can do something about getting rid of them.

LEFT **Cats relaxed and entwined, forming their own living symbol of balance and harmony.**

ABOVE **The energy and flux of the world outside your window is endlessly fascinating to your cat.**

TOP **A feline version of yin yang, embodying balance and harmony, movement and repose.**

your cat as a feng shui helper

Cats can help you to practice good feng shui in a number of ways. Perhaps it is because of their legendary ability to rout evil spirits, but cats immediately gravitate toward areas of bad or stale chi within the home and garden and set about converting it into more auspicious energy. Have you ever noticed the way a cat will immediately make a bed in an untidy drawer or closet that has been left half-open? It's the negative chi that attracts her—she simply can't resist settling down to transform it into something more positive.

BELOW Cats can help to brighten the lives of those who cannot move around very much.

RIGHT Cats unerringly find small spaces in which to fit themselves, thereby stirring up stale or trapped chi.

GOOD VIBRATIONS

Cats are wonderful generators of yang energy. Look at the way a kitten skitters around the house, darting from corner to corner. Her nimble, continuous movements stir up areas of stale chi and encourage it to disperse and circulate around the home.

And of course there are the positive benefits of the love and affection that are created whenever a cat is brought into a home. Scientific tests have proved that living together is good for both pets and people! Taking the time to relax and stroke a purring puss lowers heart rates, blood pressure, and stress levels.

Many managers of homes for the elderly, disabled, and neurologically ill have discovered the benefits cats can bring. Having the opportunity to make a fuss of a grateful cat seems to raise the spirits of the depressed and ease the distress of those suffering from mental or physical problems, or those who are not mobile. With so many good vibes being exchanged, it's no wonder the levels of chi receive a welcome boost.

BELOW Electricity is a powerful form of energy, and too much of it in one place can generate geopathic stress in your home. Although this is not good for you, your cat may find it stimulating and may seek out areas where it is at its most powerful.

GEOPATHIC STRESS

Your cat will also be drawn to any areas of geopathic stress which she finds within your home. Geopathic stress is natural radiation which emanates from the earth, and which has been distorted by modern intrusions or barriers, such as the installation of cables for communications, pipes for sewage, foundations for large buildings, and so on. Such stress can drain our energies. However, cats thrive on it! They have the innate ability to neutralize this damaging force and are by nature attracted to any sites of geopathic stress within the home. Consequently, you will find that such an area will become one of their favorite places to settle. However, be warned by their preference and don't move furniture such as a bed or a sofa into that spot. It will have an adverse effect on your health if you spend too much time in that particular location.

Equally, cats are drawn to areas of negative chi, but don't be alarmed just because your cat likes to snooze in the center of your bed, or doze in front of a radiator, or snuggle up beside you on the couch—these are not necessarily areas of negative energy. Sometimes, just like you, your cat just wants to relax in comfort and warmth. Unlike humans, cats have no qualms about self-indulgence, and it sometimes seems that they only exist to eat, play, and sleep!

identifying problem areas

LEFT **Your cat's preference for a certain sleeping spot may indicate a gathering place for negative chi.**

Areas of negative energy can draw your cat like a magnet. This explains why, when you've gone to the trouble of making your cat a comfortable bed, she refuses to use it, but insists on nestling in a messy closet every time the door is left open, or settling down in a dark, cluttered area under the stairs. It may have seemed to you that her insistence on finding her own space was just part of her natural inclination to get her own way—or downright contrariness! But she was in fact going about her work of converting negative chi into something more positive and auspicious for your home. Move her bed into one of these areas, and you'll probably find that she's happy to sleep in it—but don't be surprised if she isn't!

▌ TRACKING YOUR CAT

It's easy enough to identify these areas of negative chi. Spend a week tracking your cat's movements when she's in the house, and note where she likes to spend most of her time sitting and sleeping. Once you become aware of these areas, you will probably find other evidence of bad or stale chi. For example, you may notice that one of your cat's favorite spots is a particular corner that inexplicably tends to attract more dust than any other part of the room, or a place where plants never seem to thrive. These are all indications that this area is a focal point of negative energy.

▌ TESTING YOUR CONCLUSIONS

If your cat does tend to settle in an area that seems warm, comfortable, and welcoming, like the center of your bed or a plump, cozy armchair, there is a test you can apply to determine whether it is negative chi that is attracting her. If you can, try moving the particular piece of furniture to a different part of the room and see if she still likes to rest on it. If she ignores the furniture but goes back to the same location, the chances are that it is the negative chi that's attracting her, not comfort.

It goes without saying that once you've identified areas of bad or stale chi, you should not spend time sleeping, studying, or relaxing in them yourself. You will probably find that these areas sap your energy, and possibly your health as well, and endeavors undertaken in these areas will not prosper. Leave these areas to your cat she has very effective ways of dealing with the negative energy. If she needs any further help, you can use one of the remedies you'll read about later in this book.

ABOVE **Heaps of clutter may generate negative energy which will always attract your cat.**

BELOW **The cluttered atmosphere of this room illustrates how most living spaces could benefit from some feng shui advice.**

too many ornaments can encourage stale chi

curtains should be pulled back from windows to admit chi

lots of plants mean that the wood element has too much dominance

clearing space

Put this book down for a minute and take a long look at the room around you. Is your cat contentedly sharing a half-open, overstuffed drawer with bills and letters that are spilling out over the floor, or is she resting between untidy stacks of books on a dresser? Has she made a nest among the piles of magazines you're saving because you seem to remember that one of them features a recipe you wanted to keep? Or is she perhaps sleeping on the top shelf of the closet, lying on a sweater you bought three years ago but have never worn? Is there a vase of half-dead, cat-chewed flowers in a dusty corner, or balls of cat hair under the couch? If so, it's time to take drastic action to improve the energy flow.

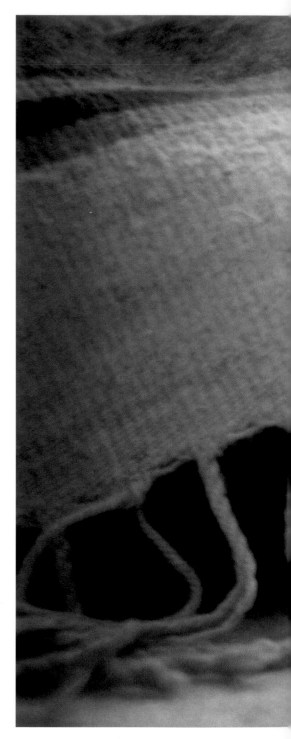

ABOVE **Your cat can only bring your attention to areas that need sorting out, such as that heap of objects you have been meaning to throw out for a month or so; the actual clearance will have to be done by you.**

A CLUTTER-FREE ZONE

While you can leave your cat to tackle specific areas of negative chi, you can't expect her to take on your entire home! You will have to do some work yourself. One of the most fundamental principles of feng shui is that your home must be kept clean and tidy—a clutter-free zone. The reason for this is that dust and dirt will sully chi, and clutter will block its progress around your home and entrap it.

COMMON SENSE

When you think about these principles, like so much about feng shui, they make perfect sense. How much time and energy do you waste looking for your keys or your checkbook when your apartment is full of junk, or a favorite sweater when your chest of drawers needs clearing out? On top of all this, dead plants or wilting flowers standing in a vase of stagnant water will generate harmful yin energy.

So it's time for a thorough spring-cleaning. Be warned: it is a good idea to shut your cat out of each room as you work on it, because all the energies being released as you start to clean out the clutter are liable to make her over-excited. You then run the risk of being so diverted by her playfulness, or so exasperated by her insistence on getting in your way, that you abandon the job halfway through! On the other hand, she might actually be happier to be out of the way if you are doing a really serious clearing out of useless objects.

ABOVE **Not in repose on the mat, but wild-eyed underneath it; sometimes the amount of negative energy your cat mops up will make her skittish.**

getting started

When you start to think about clearing up your entire house, you may find the idea so overwhelming that you don't know where to start—so you don't! If this happens, the best thing to do is to set some boundaries. Say that you will tackle just one corner—or even just one drawer—or that you will clear up for half an hour a day over the next month or so until the whole house is done. The funny thing is that once you've set these limits and gotten started, you'll probably find that you don't want to stop. As you clear your clutter, you'll become more energized and want to do more.

LET IT GO!

Be ruthless with your junk. Sort through the magazines piling up in the corner, cut out the recipe you wanted to keep, and throw the rest away. If you have books you're never likely to read again or records you don't want to listen to anymore, box them up and give them to a thrift store. If an animal charity benefits, so much the better—that means that both you and your cat have helped animals in a less fortunate situation than your pet.

Don't keep anything on display that you don't like to look at yourself or that holds unpleasant memories. If you're holding on to an ugly vase or an ornament you detest because it was given to you by a friend or relative, send that to the thrift store too. Looking at it only depletes your energy because you resent the space it takes up, and the thrift store will no doubt find a good home for it with someone who appreciates it more than you do!

CLOTHES AND ORNAMENTS

You don't have to be ruthless with objects that are useless in the practical sense but have sentimental value. Just make sure that they are put on display, if suitable, in a place where you can easily see and enjoy them. Alternatively, you can put them away carefully in a closet, where they will not clutter up your home and adversely affect the chi energy.

Try to give your wardrobe a thorough spring-clean, too. Go through your clothes with a critical eye. If you haven't worn an outfit for 12 months or more, is there really any point in holding on to it in the hope that it might come back into fashion or that you might lose a few pounds and fit into it again? And as for those buys that you liked in the store but hated as soon as you got them home—let them go!

LEFT When it comes to cleaning, take a cue from your cat's grooming methods; concentrate and proceed methodically.

ABOVE Your cat may usually be found sleeping peacefully right in the middle of whichever area you are trying to work on.

avoiding traps and pitfalls

Don't fall into the "just in case" trap. Hanging on to things "just in case" can become an excuse for never throwing anything away. If you've kept something for more than 12 months and have never used it, throw it away! While you're thinking that it might just come in handy, it's taking up valuable space and creating more excess baggage in your life.

RIGHT When your cat grooms herself, she leaves no part untreated. Follow her example by making sure you clear out every nook and cranny in and around your home to prevent bad chi from building up again.

RELEASE, REFRESH, AND ENERGIZE

If, while you're clearing up, you come across items such as a broken lamp or a rundown clock that you've been meaning to get fixed, either get them repaired or throw them away. As long as they don't work, they are just more useless clutter and may be generating negative chi. The broken lamp represents a light in your life that has gone out, the clock is an example of time standing still…

Give the house a thorough cleaning—and make sure you include those hidden corners and places like behind the back of the sofa and underneath the bed, where you hope visitors are never likely to look! These little nooks can become traps for stale chi. And don't forget your cat. Clean her bed, wash her cushion, and scrub out her food and drink-ing bowls and litter tray. Don't forget, she is a fastidious creature who doesn't appreciate a smelly bed or a bowl caked with the dried-up remains of previous meals, added to which these are further sources of bad chi.

BELOW A well-planned room allows chi to circulate freely without becoming snared by clutter.

INSIDE AND OUT

While you're clearing out your house, don't forget to tidy up and clean associated areas, such as your car, your garage, or your garden shed. You may not spend as much time in them as in your home, but they can be extra little pockets of clutter, and every time you see the mess in them your heart will sink. Each time this happens, a little more of your energy gets leached away.

While you're at it, you should also clear out the clutter that's been accumulating at the back of your mind. Write the letter, make the phone calls or fill out the official form that you've been putting off for so long. You'll find that it will be like taking a weight off your mind, and more positive thoughts will replace that persistent nagging worry!

KEEP IT UP

When your clearing session is finished, let your cat back in so you can both relax on the sofa. You'll probably be surprised to find that you don't feel as tired as you thought you would. Clearing out all your clutter will have released and refreshed the chi circulating around your home, and that in turn will have an energizing effect on you.

Once you've finished your major cleaning, keep the chi flowing. Karen Kingston, a well-respected therapist, consultant, writer, and teacher who combines feng shui principles with the art of space clearing, offers this handy tip for confirmed hoarders: whenever you acquire something new, throw out something old to make room for it. Empty trash cans and throw out newspapers and magazines every day. Clean your home regularly—and refuse to let the clutter build up.

the circular arrangement of furniture allows chi to travel easily

on entering the room, chi is diverted by a chair and begins to circulate

chi continues to flow, unimpeded by obstacles

space-clearing rituals

If you've just moved into a new house or apartment, do you find that your cat gets more "spooked" than she used to? Or does she suddenly seem to stare into space, as if she's watching something you can't see, or even arch her back and start hissing? Are you yourself finding it a little hard to get settled? Do you sometimes feel that, although your new home suits your requirements perfectly, something isn't quite right?

RESIDUAL ENERGY

As well as using feng shui to create a haven in your new home, you might also want to consider "space clearing." This is not actually a part of traditional feng shui, but is related to it in principle. It has evolved through a number of ancient cultures, and many practitioners claim to have found it effective in reinforcing the effects of feng shui.

Both feng shui and space-clearing experts have observed that when a married couple move into a home which has become available because its previous occupants got divorced, the new couple often end up splitting up too. The reason for this, the experts believe, is that the departing couple leave behind residual energy of the conflict between them, and this then affects the next occupants. Similarly, bad health or misfortune may seem to plague a home, no matter who lives in it. Space clearing can help to get rid of these bad vibes and fill the new home with auspicious energy. It can also be used to clear and revitalize chi in your home, no matter how long you've lived there.

WHAT YOU WILL NEED

Space clearing has its own rituals, and there are a number of excellent books to tell you how to do it, including those written by Karen Kingston,

Sarah Shurety, and Denise Linn (see *Further Reading, p. 157*). The procedure is quite straightforward and involves little cost, aside from purchasing a few items like rock salt, incense or essential oils, and a bell.

Once again, it is probably best to keep your cat out of the room while you are space clearing. It is considered more effective to be alone while you are doing it anyway, and your cat may be disturbed or distressed by the changes taking place in the levels of energy.

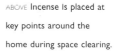

ABOVE Incense is placed at key points around the home during space clearing.

essential oils can be used in the place of incense, or to freshen the house after space clearing

bells are used to chase away bad spirits

rock or sea salt is often sprinkled on the threshold of the house

LEFT A "spooked" cat may be reacting to residual energy left in a home by its previous occupants.

RIGHT The ingredients needed for space clearing. Such ceremonies occur in many ancient traditions.

2.

creature
comforts and
harmonious
homes

同心的貓
与
健康的家

different cats, different homes

You may have chosen your cat from a litter of kittens or got her from an animal protection organization. But does she want to live with you? You'll soon find out, because cats are notoriously independent creatures, and if their current home doesn't suit them, they will quickly move to somewhere that does—and a new owner.

EACH ONE AN INDIVIDUAL

All cats are different, just as people are. Some like the noise and hurly-burly of life in a family with young children; others prefer a quieter, more sedate existence. Some settle happily into a home with other cats or even dogs; others like to rule the roost as their owner's only pet.

Be careful about making any changes to your cat's life. An acquaintance of mine couldn't resist acquiring a new cat every few months or so. In the end, she had six—far too many for her small apartment. The cats fought constantly because they didn't have enough space to establish their own territories within the home or find their specific areas of negative chi. Then she added a puppy into the mix—with disastrous results. The cats seemed to make a unanimous decision to leave: one by one, over the next few months, they quietly moved on, leaving my acquaintance with just the eldest cat, who was presumably too old to consider relocating.

THE UNEXPECTED CAT

A story with a happier ending concerns a single friend of mine who recently started to share a cat belonging to a family living a few doors away. Most of the day, the cat enjoys the company of the children, but in the evenings or when he wants a break from all that yang energy, he simply moves down the street to watch television with my friend and her two other cats. The two households split feeding and vet's bills between them, and everyone, including the cat, is happy!

It is astonishing how cats seem to gravitate toward the right owner for them. Another acquaintance was at a very low ebb when her cat found her. She had been having health and work problems and became even more depressed when she heard that a friend of hers had been involved in an accident. The day after she got this news, a cat appeared on her kitchen windowsill. She ignored him for a while, but after he had been meowing outside for an hour, she finally gave in and let him in. He immediately wound himself around her legs, demanding attention. She fed him—and he hasn't left her house since! It seems likely that he was attracted by all the negative chi within the house. Despite being a stray, he is a particularly affectionate and loving cat, and my friend's life has certainly improved since he arrived.

ABOVE **A relaxed cat, responding blissfully to her owner's touch, has obviously found a home that is just right for her.**

LEFT Some cats prefer to move freely between two or three home bases, sharing their talents among several owners.

45

happy cats

Unless your cat is happy within your home, she cannot do her work of converting negative chi into something more beneficial. A cat who is sick or miserable will only add to the negative chi in the home. So unless you are sure that you are ready for the responsibility of keeping a cat happy, healthy, and well cared for, don't make the commitment of taking her into your home. (Incidentally, this also applies to any other pet.)

ABOVE **However old and sleepy your cat is, she will still be a potent force for good in the home, neutralizing or transforming negative energy.**

RIGHT **The picture of contentment, a happy cat basks in her favorite spot. It is up to you to keep her warm, safe, and well-fed; in return for this she will radiate positive energy from which you will benefit.**

▌KEEPING YOUR CAT CONTENTED

Your cat's welfare should be paramount. Give her plenty of love and attention, feed her regularly, and make sure she always has plenty to drink. Keep her food bowls, bedding, and litter tray clean, have her vaccinated regularly, and take her to the vet at the first sign of illness.

Learn to identify your cat's needs and to recognize the signs she gives that she is hungry, upset, unwell, or in pain, so that you can quickly sort out any problems. In the end, you will benefit from this concern as much as your pet— the fitter and livelier she is, the brighter and happier the atmosphere in your home will be.

That doesn't mean that when your cat gets old, you should replace her with a younger one. Even if she is no longer as lively as she used to be and tends to sleep most of the day, she is still neutralizing harmful chi with the love and affection she generates. As long as she is not sick or in pain, she deserves to live out her days in peace and contentment.

▌INTRODUCING NEWCOMERS

If there are going to be any new additions to your household—for example, if you are expecting a baby or planning to bring in another cat or other pet—introduce your cat to the newcomer gradually. Give her plenty of reassurance and make sure she knows that she is still the number one cat in your life. Without that reassurance, she might just move on to a household where she feels more appreciated!

design implications

Okay, so you've got a happy cat and you've given your house a thorough spring-cleaning. But there's a lot more to feng shui than that! Don't think that just by clearing out all the clutter from your home, you will have dispelled all the bad chi. We've already seen how important location is; in fact, the very structure of your home also affects the quality of chi within it and the way that it circulates around the house.

LEFT **If your cat always seeks out a certain spot on your bed, perhaps it is time to take a fresh look at its placement in the room.**

BELOW **Many cats quickly learn how to manipulate their environment and may use their skills to show you what needs to be done.**

IMPORTANT FEATURES

Feng shui experts consider buildings that are square, rectangular (provided they are not too narrow), circular, or octagonal to be the most auspicious. L-shaped, U-shaped, or irregularly shaped houses are thought to be less lucky, although certain remedies can go a long way toward correcting their deficiencies. Your home's individual features also have a big influence on the chi within it. The height of the ceilings, the size and shape of the windows and doors, the location and nature of staircases, and the positioning of furniture are all significant.

Many of the theories about how the structure of your home affects chi have a grounding in common sense. For example, feng shui experts believe that low ceilings bear down on chi so that it cannot circulate—and who hasn't felt, on entering a room with a low ceiling, a sense of claustrophobia and almost a need to duck your head, as though the ceiling were falling down on you? By following the advice of feng shui experts, you can help to dispel those feelings.

MAKE USE OF YOUR CAT

If you watch the way your cat reacts to the different features of your home, you can learn to spot troublesome areas. Which window does she prefer to sit in? Does she like to sleep in the hall or on the stairs? Does she often curl up in the same place on your bed?

As you become more familiar with the principles of feng shui, you will start to look around your home with "feng shui eyes" and be able to recognize potential trouble spots by yourself. Because the fact is, you can't leave it all up to your cat. If you do, and she tries to transmute all the negative chi in the house on her own, she's going to become overloaded. This will in turn make her ill—or, at the very least, unhappy.

THE SHAPE OF BUILDINGS

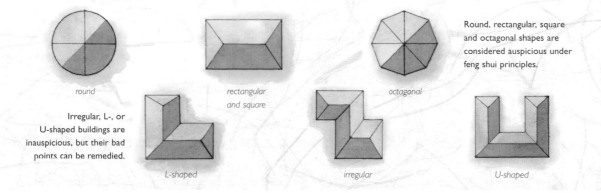

round

rectangular and square

octagonal

Round, rectangular, square and octagonal shapes are considered auspicious under feng shui principles.

Irregular, L-, or U-shaped buildings are inauspicious, but their bad points can be remedied.

L-shaped

irregular

U-shaped

structural remedies

Fortunately, there are many ways in which you can help your cat sort out the negative chi within your home. Between the two of you, you should be able to maintain a healthy, harmonious, and well-balanced environment that will benefit not only you, but everyone who shares your space.

RIGHT The plant in the corner of the room helps to dispel any stagnant chi that might collect there. Owners and cat are able to relax in the harmonious atmosphere that results.

ABOVE Mirrors can be used to amplify good chi and deflect bad influences. Get advice before you place them to make sure you do not amplify the bad energies by mistake.

KEEP THINGS SIMPLE

You may have heard horror stories about feng shui consultants recommending expensive and disruptive structural changes to people's homes. But such drastic alterations aren't necessary. There are some relatively cheap and simple remedies that you can use to help make up for any deficiencies in the structure of your home.

You will learn more about the common remedies in Part 3, but those listed below are the ones most often used to correct faults.

LIGHT Light is very important in helping chi to circulate properly and stopping it from going stale in dark corners. Natural light is always best, but where there is none, artificial lighting can be helpful, too. Fix dimmer switches to control the amount of brightness in a room, and shade lights so that the bulbs do not show, as this is considered to be inauspicious. Candles are also a good source of light for feng shui purposes, but

make sure they are never left unattended, particularly when your cat is around. Cats can be very careless with the tips of their tails!

PLANTS Plants freshen chi and also generate their own, and they can be very helpful in deflecting poison arrows within the home. Make sure that plants are kept healthy and well-watered. If they start to die, throw them away and replace them.

MIRRORS Mirrors can be used to deflect sha chi and may act as a remedy in unpleasant areas, such as the toilet. They also stimulate chi by reflecting natural light. By placing mirrors in a position where they will reflect a pleasing outside view into a room, you can help to draw healthy chi into your home.

WIND CHIMES Wind chimes can be helpful in slowing down sha chi and also in diverting chi in a different direction. The movement of mobiles has a similar effect.

CRYSTALS Crystals can introduce more light into a room or a dark corner. If they are hung up by a ribbon, the movement created as they catch the breeze will help to reinforce the remedy, and your cat will enjoy the patterns of light that they cast around the room.

ELECTRICAL DEVICES Household devices such as televisions, stereos, electric clocks, food mixers, and so on can all help to stimulate chi, but these are very potent remedies, so use them with care.

RIGHT Living plants are always good feng shui, but they should be well looked after so that they can do their job efficiently. Try to avoid dried plants.

doors

The front door of your home (meaning your street door if you live in a house, or the entrance to your own living space if you're an apartment dweller) symbolizes your relationship with the outside world, so it's important to keep it freshly painted and generally in good repair. Your door is also where visitors enter, and you should do whatever you can to make it look welcoming. Of course, there are few things more welcoming than a contented cat purring on the doorstep!

ATTRACTING CHI

If possible, your door should be made of solid wood; too much glass in the front door makes the house's occupants vulnerable. It should open easily (without creaking!) and be well lit from the outside. The doorbell should be in working order and make an attractive sound, and the path and/or steps leading to the door should be clean and free of clutter or obstacles. No one wants to be confronted with an ugly, smelly trash can as they approach your home!

A pair of round-leafed, flowering bushes planted on either side of the door helps to attract chi into the home. Never plant trees in this location, though, since they symbolize the joss sticks that the Chinese customarily leave at the entrances to tombs.

LEFT An almost perfect front door in feng shui terms: solid wood, handsome proportions, bracketed by round-leaved bushes and guarded by a large, composed cat.

THE IDEAL DOORWAY

The proportions of the front door are important, as it is the main route by which chi enters the home. If it is too large, it admits too much chi, which may overwhelm the occupants. The remedy for this is to paint the hall in dark colors or to place a heavy object near the door to stabilize the chi. If your front door is too small, it squeezes the chi and doesn't let in enough. You can counteract this by positioning a mirror over the door, or on both sides of it, to make it look bigger.

Doors also have a bearing on the flow of chi within your home. A particularly harmful situation occurs when the front door of the house is immediately opposite the back door; this means that chi immediately escapes out of the back door before it can circulate around the home. Feng shui consultants believe that this results in opportunities disappearing before the home's occupants have the chance to grasp them. Hanging a wind chime or crystal between the two doors can help to disperse chi around the house. For a more potent remedy, you could place a physical barrier between the two doors, such as a screen or a large plant.

Inside the house, a line of internal doors in a row together will cause sha chi. Again, the wind chime or crystal remedy can help.

windows

According to feng shui principles, windows should always open outward, not inward, in order for chi to circulate properly. Casement windows are considered preferable to sash windows because they open wider to let chi into the room. Needless to say, windows should be cleaned regularly, so that chi is not sullied as it enters your home.

ABOVE **Very inauspicious:** sash windows with long straight curtains blocking the entry of chi. This cat has a lot of work to do.

RIGHT **Four cats cluster** around this inauspicious pointed window; their presence is needed to block off the poison arrow.

▌ CRYSTALS AND CURVES

Crystals are a particularly good remedy to use in less-than-perfect windows. Hang them where they can catch the sun and the breeze, so that they give you the benefits of both light and movement—and make sure they are out of reach of inquisitive cats' paws!

As you will now be aware, an unpleasant feature outside your window, such as a prison or a piece of wasteland, will generate harmful chi. To prevent it from entering your home, place a small mirror on the windowsill, facing outward, to deflect this bad energy. Plants on the windowsill will also help to counteract it, and of course your cat won't need much persuasion to sit there and keep an eye on the outside world, protecting your home from harm at the same time.

▌ MAXIMIZING LIGHT

If your cat is anything like mine, she sees straight curtains as a constant challenge and loves to climb up them until she reaches the curtain rail—and then abseil back down again, using her claws as brakes! It's her way of counteracting the straight lines that speed up chi. It's preferable to have curtains that reach the floor and hang in curves, or that can be looped back when they are open to form a nice undulating line. It should be possible to draw curtains right back from the window to allow maximum chi and light to enter the room.

As you will learn in Part 4, the Form School of feng shui maintains that the west side of a house is governed by your cat's larger cousin,

ABOVE **To remedy** inauspicious windows, hang a crystal in front of the window (on the inside) where it can catch the light.

the tiger, which is both powerful and unpredictable. Whether you believe this or not, it's certainly true that the afternoon sun can be glaring. Consequently, the Chinese often leave the curtains on west-facing windows drawn at all times, or they may even block the window off altogether! A less drastic solution is, once again, to hang a crystal in the window, to split the invading rays of the sun and send colored patterns of light spinning around the room.

beams and ceilings

Although many people in the West love to have traditional exposed beams in their houses, in feng shui terms, beams are really bad news! This is because they speed up chi as it passes along their straight lines. They can also have an oppressive effect on the house's occupants—the Chinese believe they can be harmful to one's health. So if your cat loves to perch on an open beam inside your home, she's not just getting a good view of what's going on—she's also trying to protect you by transmuting the beam's harmful influence.

BALANCING BEAMS

Beams should be avoided most particularly in the bedroom. Feng shui practitioners believe that having a bed positioned under a beam can cause a number of ailments, depending on which part of the body is overshadowed as the person lies in bed. For example, if the beam runs over the head of the bed, it can cause headaches; a beam over the middle of the bed can cause stomach problems; and so on. If the beam "divides" a couple by running over the center of the bed, it's said that it can cause marital break-ups.

LEFT **A fluffy cat, apparently half asleep, effortlessly softens the straight line of a sofa arm.**

BELOW **Exposed timber beams are considered to be bad feng shui because they funnel chi out of the room.**

In kitchens and dining rooms, beams are believed to cause money problems, and no one should ever try to work while sitting under a beam—it can have a draining effect on physical and mental vitality.

BEAM REMEDIES

However, if you really can't avoid having open beams in your home, then you will be relieved to learn that there are feng shui remedies to counteract their potentially harmful effects, even in the bedroom. To encourage chi to flow around the room, fix bamboo flutes to the beam at an angle, with their mouthpieces pointing downward, to mimic the upper left and right sides of the pa kua (see pp. 84–85). Or you can attach ornamental fans to the beams, using red ribbon to increase the remedy's potency. Swathing the beam in fabric or arranging fabric over your bed mosquito-net-style are also effective—although if you're claustrophobic you may find a net almost as oppressive as the beam. (There's also the risk that your cat may think you've treated her to some kind of feline adventure playground!) The oppressive feeling caused by low beams can also be lightened by painting them white.

Low ceilings can also have a depressing effect on a house's occupants and may cause bad headaches. Alleviate their effects by putting up mirrors to make the room look bigger, and position lighting so that it shines upward.

ABOVE **A small ornamental fan attached to an offending beam can do a lot to dispel the harmful chi it generates.**

staircases

Does your cat like to sit on the stairs? If so, she may be indicating that all is not well with the passage of chi in that location. Ideally, stairs should be wide, well lit, and curved. But sadly, not many of us have homes that allow for such palatial staircases! Instead, in many houses the upstairs landing has a low ceiling which appears to bear down on the top of the stairs, compressing the flow of chi. However, you can "raise" such a ceiling by hanging a mirror on it.

ABOVE **A trailing plant can help prevent chi rushing down a spiral staircase and out of the front door.**

ABOVE Shining light upwards can combat the cramped atmosphere which may be caused by low ceilings.

RIGHT This inauspicious flight of stairs requires the energy of three cats, one on each tread.

WINDING OR STRAIGHT?

With all its curving lines, a spiral staircase might seem the best kind to have—but, in fact, feng shui experts say this is the worst kind of staircase! According to them, a spiral staircase "bores through" the home like a giant drill. When a cat sits on a winding staircase, then, she isn't just being decorative—she is actually hard at work neutralizing its negative effects!

If your home does have a spiral staircase, don't despair or start making expensive structural changes. Instead, try putting a strong light at the top of the stairs, so that it illuminates them from top to bottom. If the steps are open, with no risers, they could allow chi to escape through the gaps. To remedy this, place a large plant on the floor behind the bottom stairs, in the center of the spiral; this will encourage the chi to move upward.

CONSERVING CHI

The Chinese also believe that it is very unlucky to have a staircase that runs directly to the front door, as feng shui experts say that this allows luck and wealth to flow straight out of the house. To compensate for this, hang a crystal ball or wind chime between the stairs and the door, or place a large plant there. Alternatively, you could hang a convex mirror on the back of the front door to deflect some of the chi away from it. Having a staircase that is rounded at the bottom will also help to turn chi away from the door and conserve its energy.

the hall

Imagine that you are a visitor to your home. What sort of impression do you receive when you walk into the hall? Is it bright and welcoming? Or do you trip over the cat as you grope your way through the gloom?

Most of the chi that enters your home comes in through your front door. Therefore, the hall is the first room it encounters and the place from which chi finds its way around the rest of your house. If your cat does tend to frequent your hall, it may mean that chi is encountering obstacles in gaining access to your home.

WELCOMING CHI

A hall that is light, warm, and welcoming will encourage chi to enter. A "Welcome" mat just inside the door will be another incentive, and it is said that placing three gold coins under the doormat will bring good luck. (You can buy three Chinese coins tied with a lucky red ribbon from a number of feng shui suppliers.)

If your hall is only just big enough to let the door swing open, so that you are immediately confronted by a wall, there is an instant obstacle as soon as chi enters your home. Remedy this by putting a mirror on the wall facing the door. (The mirror remedy is a good one to use in any cramped space, not just your entry hall.) Or try hanging a picture of an attractive landscape opposite the door. The picture should be one that leads the eye into it, thus giving the impression of greater depth. It is especially important to keep a small hall well lit by a bright overhead light.

CALMING CHI

If you have a long, thin hallway, you may find that your cat likes to sit at the end of it. This is because sha chi rushes down its length. The energy can be calmed and slowed down by hanging a mobile or a wind chime from the ceiling in the center of the hall, or by putting some bushy, round-leafed plants at intervals along it. Another way of slowing down fast-rushing chi is to place mirrors at regular intervals down the hall. It's thought that the chi will bounce back and forth from one mirror to the next, so its direct route down the corridor is interrupted before it can rush into the other rooms of the house.

ABOVE The cramped energy in a small hall can be relieved by hanging a picture of an auspicious landscape on the wall— rolling hills and water are a particularly good choice.

LEFT Placing lucky Chinese coins underneath your doormat will attract wealth.

LEFT Like mirrors and crystals, wind chimes are a useful remedy in places where the energy flow needs to be moderated.

FAR LEFT You may often discover your cat sitting at the end of a long dark hall. This is because she is busy absorbing sha chi.

the kitchen

Why is it that whenever you are trying to cook an elaborate meal, your cat decides to wind herself around your legs and generally get in the way as you move around the kitchen? She's not just demanding attention—or morsels of food that you might accidentally drop! She is also excited by the amount of energy being created, because in feng shui terms, the kitchen is the hub of the home. Food and its preparation are associated with wealth—the more money you have, the better you can eat, and the better you eat, the more energy you have to make money.

ENERGY AND MOVEMENT

In the healthiest houses, the kitchen is always a hive of activity. Just think of the energy created by different sources during food preparation: the heat from naked flames; the movement of water flowing from the faucet; the clatter of cooking utensils and the whirring of electrical equipment—not to mention the exertions of the chef! And most kitchen units are arranged in straight lines along the walls of the kitchen, accelerating the flow of all that chi.

If anything, the chi in the kitchen usually needs to be slowed down, rather than refreshed, although you should still, of course, look around for corners where it can get trapped. By keeping your cat's feeding bowls in the kitchen, along with her bed, you might be able to persuade her to sleep in there more often and help to calm the chi down.

BELOW She may look as though she is simply enjoying a meal, but this cat is hard at work calming kitchen chi.

KITCHEN CLEANLINESS

Needless to say, just as your kitchen should be kept spotless and dirty dishes should not be allowed to accumulate in the sink for days on end, your cat's feeding bowls should also be kept immaculately clean. If she doesn't appear to be hungry and hasn't finished her meal within a few hours, don't leave the food to get stale and smelly—throw it away. Similarly, keep her water or milk bowl clean and freshly filled, and don't let the contents get stale or curdled.

ABOVE Straight lines amplify the energy in any kitchen. Your cat's calming presence will help to control the flow in this very yang area.

RIGHT Cats will eat together as long as the bowl gives them enough space. Fighting cats generate bad energy.

It is not, however, a good idea to keep your cat's litter tray in the kitchen. If possible, move it to a place like a screened porch or even into your own bathroom. Better still, if possible, don't have a litter tray in the house at all. If you have a backyard, cultivate an area of rough earth masked by bushes and encourage your cat to use that as her toilet.

the bathroom

According to feng shui experts, bathrooms are likely to be a problem area in any house. Pre-modern-day Chinese homes did not have bathrooms. The toilet area was kept outside the home, so people would have considered it inauspicious to have it under their roof.

ABOVE **Plants are excellent remedies for any feng shui problems you may discover in your bathroom.**

A YIN AREA

For rather obvious reasons of modesty, the Chinese traditionally consider it most unlucky to have a toilet that immediately faces the bathroom door. If yours does, hang a wind chime between the door and the toilet.

It is also considered unlucky for the bathroom to be the first thing you see when you walk in the front door. If this is the case in your home, keep the bathroom door closed at all times. You might also consider hanging a mirror on the outside of the bathroom door. (If you keep your cat's litter box in the bathroom, you may have to install a cat flap in the door, so that she can get in and out to use it.)

The bathroom is a very yin area, because of its association with water, so furnishings and decoration should be kept simple, leaving little space for chi to go stale and cause damp and fungus stains. Plants are a good remedy to use in bathrooms to improve the chi.

CHI AND WATER

Because of the bathroom's yin nature, it's unlikely that, as a yin animal herself, your cat will spend much time in there. When she does visit, you'll probably find that she is fascinated by the running water, especially if you have a dripping faucet in the bathtub or sink. (By the way, as the water runs down the waste pipe, it represents a drain on the chi in the room, so make sure any faulty washers are replaced promptly.)

Some feng shui practitioners recommend leaving sink and bath plugs in the plughole when they are not being used, to prevent the chi from leaking away. Similarly, the lid of the toilet should always be left down, so that the chi doesn't use that as an escape route. (If the author had known this a few years ago, an unfortunate incident could have been avoided. Her cat, walking around the rim of a filling bathtub, lost her balance and fell in. Shocked, she leapt out in a single bound—only to land in the toilet bowl!)

LEFT **Cats usually find bathrooms too yin, but they are always attracted to water and so they may like to join you and keep guard as you soak in the tub.**

FAR LEFT **The toilet bowl is a troublesome area in feng shui terms, as it represents the flushing away of energy. Keep the lid down when it is not in use.**

65

the bedroom

In feng shui terms, bedrooms are the place for rest and recharging the batteries, and remedies should be used sparingly in this room, perhaps only to slow down sha chi. The room's furnishings should be aimed at promoting relaxation and a good night's sleep, which means that anything connected with work, such as a computer, has no place here.

ABOVE **Your cat will be attracted to your bed; encourage her to sleep in an enrichment area instead.**

FAR RIGHT **Kittens are full of yang energy and may cause excitement in what should be a relaxing room.**

BELOW **Cats are too restless to be good sleeping companions for humans.**

A RESTFUL HAVEN

The need for rest and relaxation also means that you should perhaps consider banning your cat from your bedroom at night. Yes, of course she likes to sleep on your bed—but how often is your sleep disturbed because she is nestled in the small of your back and you can't roll over? How many times are you awakened long before the alarm goes off because your cat decides that it's time for breakfast and jumps on your face? Besides, if your cat can be persuaded to sleep in one of your enrichment areas (you'll read more about these in Part 3), she can be helping you while she sleeps by generating good energy in a particular direction.

BEDROOM RULES

Your cat is not the only potent remedy which should be banned from the bedroom. Other popular remedies, such as plants, create too much yang energy, and water remedies are considered potentially harmful. We have already looked at the bad influence exerted by beams, particularly in the bedroom (*see pp. 56–57*), so you know that you should avoid putting your bed under one. But you should also be aware that built-in cupboards with overhead compartments and four-poster beds can have a similar effect. In fact, overhead cupboards are said to cause headaches.

Spare no expense in making your bed as comfortable as you can to ensure that you are fully rested. And give some thought to the bed's position in the room. According to feng shui practice, when you are lying in bed, your feet should not point directly at the door. This is an inauspicious position, because, according to Chinese tradition, dead people are always carried out of bedrooms feet first.

You should not have any mirrors directly facing the bed, so that you can see your reflection in them when you sit up—they can cause insomnia and bad dreams. This also applies to television screens. (The energy produced by a television set is not conducive to rest, so ideally you shouldn't have one in the bedroom.) If you feel you really can't do without a mirror or the television in your bedroom—or you don't want to rip out those mirrored cupboards!—turn them away from the bed or cover them with fabric before you go to sleep.

the living room

Although scientists have claimed that cats cannot actually perceive anything on the screen, television sets nevertheless seem to hold a special fascination for them. Many cats seem to like settling on top of the set—especially if they can drape a tail in front of the screen while you're trying to watch your favorite program!

THE CENTER OF ATTENTION

It's not just the heat of the set that attracts cats to the top of the TV. All electrical devices are potent sources of energy, and the television is particularly powerful because it becomes the focus of attention as soon as it is switched on. With the pictures it projects, it also brings the outside world into the home.

In most Western homes, the television is the focal point of the living room, and the armchairs are arranged to give everyone a good view. In the pre-soap days of ancient China, however, the center of the main living room was the warmth-giving fire. If you have a fireplace, even if it now houses an artificial fire, you should try to restore that as the focal point of the room, with chairs arranged around it.

TURN OFF THE TELEVISION

Don't keep the television on out of habit. Switch it on only when there's a program that you particularly want to watch. The rest of the time, if possible, keep it out of sight in a cupboard or cabinet. It will be healthier for you, and, as your cat won't be tempted to settle on top of the set, it will also be better for your television! Needless to say, your cat won't need much encouragement to stretch out in front of the fire once it has been made the central feature of the room.

Whether you have a fireplace or not, try to arrange the furniture in the octagonal pattern of the pa kua (*see pp. 84–85*). This will enable chi to flow more smoothly, whereas arranging furniture in straight lines around the walls of the

FAR LEFT Your cat will be attracted to the living room as it is the central point in the house, a place where she can be sure of getting attention if she wants it.

room will accelerate it. The head of the household, or whoever uses the room most, should have what the Chinese considered to be the "honored guest" seat—the chair facing the door, which allows them to see anyone entering the room before they themselves are seen. For the sake of hospitality, this chair should also be given to any guest visiting the house—even if it does mean tossing your cat out of it!

ABOVE The fireplace should be the focus of a comfortable living room.

BELOW Arrange your furniture in an octagonal pattern; this will allow chi to circulate freely.

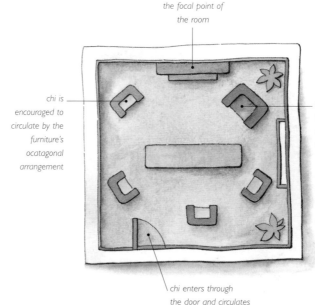

the fireplace is the focal point of the room

chi is encouraged to circulate by the furniture's octagonal arrangement

the head of the household sits facing the doorway

chi enters through the door and circulates around the room

the dining room

When considering improving the feng shui of your dining room, think of the kind of room you would like to be welcomed into as a guest. Keep the words "comfort" and "relaxation" in mind and you won't go too far wrong.

ABOVE **A mirror in the dining area is a good idea as it "doubles" the amount of food in the room, and so encourages abundance.**

BELOW **When seating your guests, make sure that the "most honored" guest sits facing the door, or can see the door in a mirror.**

SPACE AND ABUNDANCE

As this is a yin room, you should cultivate a relaxed atmosphere here, but not as relaxed as, say, the bedroom—otherwise, your guests will be nodding off over their dinner!

You will want to give the impression of spaciousness in the dining room, so use uplighters to "raise" the ceiling and mirrors to make the room look bigger. It is considered particularly auspicious to use mirrors to reflect the food on the table, as the reflection "doubles" the quantity available, and the Chinese associate food with wealth. However, make sure that you position the mirrors so that you can see all of yourself in them—it is considered very inauspicious if a mirror "beheads" you.

Here, as in the living room, when you are entertaining visitors, the most important guest should face the door. If this is not possible, he or she should at least be able to see the door in a strategically placed mirror.

ABOVE **Octagonal tables are the most auspicious. If you have one, your cat will probably confirm this by sitting in the middle of it.**

RIGHT **Welcome cats into the dining room (they will come in anyway); their presence brings energy and abundance to the space.**

AUSPICIOUS OCTAGONS

The best shape for a dining room table is octagonal, but a circular one or a rectangular one with rounded corners would also be good. Make sure that the table is big enough to comfortably accommodate everyone who will sit around it. Having plenty of space increases the atmosphere of wealth and abundance—and nobody wants someone else's elbow in their ribs while they're eating!

Lighting should not be too bright. Install dimmer switches so the lighting is adjustable—and of course, there is much to be said for using candles on the table, which will energize chi both in the room and in your guests. Fresh flowers used as a table decoration also help to energize chi, but make sure that the water is kept clear and fresh and that any wilting blooms are removed immediately. The arrangement should not be so big that it acts as a barrier in the center of the table, causing division between those sitting around it. It is also inadvisable to have clocks in the dining room because you should be eating at a relaxed pace and should not feel hurried by the passing of time.

poison arrows

You've already seen in Part I how poison arrows are caused by the rooflines or corners of adjoining houses pointing at your own. Just as they exist outside the house, there can also be poison arrows, or "sharp knives" as they are sometimes called, that can threaten you within it.

SOFTENING CORNERS

If your cat likes to sit in an awkward spot, you might find that she is trying to protect you from a poison arrow pointing in that direction. Those that are caused by protruding corners can be deflected by putting a mirror on the wall on either side of the corner, or by placing a large plant there, or hanging a crystal in front of it. An angular column in the room can be softened by hanging mirrors on each of its sides, or by encouraging a climbing plant to grow around it. Circular columns are not a problem, since their shape encourages chi to flow around them.

When you are buying new furniture, you can help to avoid poison arrows by choosing furniture that has rounded edges. Where problems crop up with existing furniture, move the pieces so that they are not pointing directly at the places where you or your family like to sit. Or you can cover them with a throw or place a plant in front of them. However, it is not good feng shui practice to have plants in the bedroom, so if you have any poison arrows pointing at your bed, neutralize them by hanging a wind chime in front of the offending corner.

SHELVES AND DOORS

Around the house, don't leave cabinet doors open so that they point at you—this also creates poison arrows. Another common source is open shelves and open bookcases. It's better to put doors on them, but if this is not possible, cultivate a plant with leaves that will trail over the shelves, or place a crystal on the shelves to dilute the effect of the arrow.

Poison arrows can be difficult for your cat to combat, unless she always positions herself between you and the offending corner. However, once you become aware of them, you will soon be able to put them right.

ABOVE Handsome plants can be used effectively to screen off corners, soften the poison arrows they generate, and prevent stagnant chi from collecting.

FAR LEFT Young cats will spend a lot of time chasing their own tails up and down the stairs and entwining themselves around banisters. They are having fun and at the same time they are absorbing the poison arrow energy generated by the straight lines of the stairs.

pictures in the sitting room should ideally feature peaceful or relaxing subjects

encouraging a trailing plant to grow around this pole would soften its effect on chi

softly draped curtains would help to moderate the flow of chi

this plant blocks off an awkward corner, but one with round leaves would be even more effective

LEFT Once you have learned to look around a room with "feng shui eyes" you will soon spot areas which are ripe for improvement.

3

staying healthy and happy with feng shui

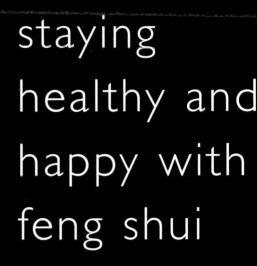

luck

In the West, we tend to think of luck as something that strikes randomly, out of the blue. We talk about "Lady Luck" smiling on us, "a lucky break," or "lucking out," as if fortune, good or bad, is something quite outside our control. The ancient Chinese, however, took a different, and rather more spiritual, view of luck.

THE LUCK TRIANGLE

To begin with, the ancient Chinese believed that there were three different kinds of luck. These are "heaven luck," "earth luck," and "humankind luck."

Heaven luck is close to the Western view of fate. It is something you are born with; it is laid down in your Chinese horoscope, and its effects are inescapable.

Earth luck is luck generated by the kind of environment in which you live—opportunities and changes that come your way and enable you to achieve your goals. However, by itself, earth luck is not enough for you to achieve the optimum satisfaction from life. It has to be coupled with humankind luck, which is brought about by your own initiative and hard work— in other words, luck that you make for yourself. And yet, while humankind luck insists that you

must make a considerable effort on your own behalf, at the same time, it is considered wrong to be single-minded in the pursuit of your ambitions. For humankind luck to be most effective, you must also find time to consider and help those less fortunate than you, perhaps by aiding them with feng shui.

LUCK AND FENG SHUI

Feng shui fits into the luck triangle by helping you to increase the quality of your earth luck. It does this by bringing positive and beneficial influences to bear on your life and encouraging fortunate opportunities to come your way. And when you do encounter some of the pitfalls you will inevitably meet through your preordained heaven luck, feng shui can help to soften their effect and make it easier for you to cope with them satisfactorily.

ABOVE In the West, the cat is considered to be a bearer of luck. Opinion is divided on whether it is good or bad, especially in the case of black cats. Most owners consider themselves lucky to be able to share their lives with a cat of any color.

FAR LEFT Cats have a lot to teach us about seizing the moment. Observe the bright eyes, alert pose, and forward-pointing ears: this cat is about to pounce on something that will brighten up her day.

LEFT A cat basks in the center of a fanciful representation of the luck triangle. Most cats make it their business to seek out luck rather than waiting for it to find them.

luck and feng shui

The **Compass School** of feng shui believes that there are eight fundamental areas of your life in which feng shui can help to encourage good luck. These are known as the eight aspirations or enrichments, and their characteristics are outlined in the diagram below.

RIGHT Two potential luck-bringers sitting in one basket; all they need is a push in the right direction.

THE EIGHT ENRICHMENTS

SOUTHEAST
WEALTH
Obvious!

SOUTH
FAME
Your standing in the world and the way in which you are perceived by other people.

SOUTHWEST
LOVE LIFE
Even more obvious!

EAST
FAMILY
This relates to the health of your family, and to your relationships with members of your family.

WEST
CHILDREN
Relating specifically to your children, as well as your children's achievements.

NORTHEAST
EDUCATION
Not just academic achievement, but also how you increase your knowledge and self-development.

NORTH
CAREER
Relating to success in your work, however you choose to define it.

NORTHWEST
HELPFUL PEOPLE
These include teachers or mentors in your workplace—anyone who helps you to get the most out of your life.

THE ELEMENT COLORS

As you learned in Part 1, each of the elements is associated with a particular color, which also appears within the pa kua. These colors also apply to the enrichment areas with which each element is linked:

 WATER *black, blue*

 FIRE *red*

 WOOD *green, brown*

 METAL *silver, gold, white*

 EARTH *yellow, brown*

five elements

Once you start applying the basic principles of **Compass School** feng shui to your home, you will need to understand one more bit of theory before you can start using effective remedies to enhance chi energy.

ELEMENTS AND ENRICHMENTS

You will remember how, when we were talking about yin and yang in Part I, we explained that they were based on five elements, which are the universe's main energies—fire, metal, water, wood, and earth. These elements also relate to the luck or enrichment areas, as shown in the diagram below.

SOUTH
FAME, FIRE

SOUTHEAST
WEALTH, WOOD

SOUTHWEST
LOVE LIFE, EARTH

EAST
FAMILY, WOOD

WEST
CHILDREN, METAL

NORTHEAST
EDUCATION, EARTH

NORTHWEST
HELPFUL PEOPLE, METAL

CAREER, WATER
NORTH

ABOVE **In physical repose but on full mental alert, this cat sniffs the breeze to discover in which direction the wind of luck is blowing.**

LEFT **The element and enrichment wheel shows which one of the five elements and which direction are associated with the various areas of your life. Judicious use of the right element in the relevant location will help to enrich those areas.**

FAR LEFT **Cats are associated with the wood element, and will often single it out when recharging their batteries.**

productive and destructive cycles

The five elements can be arranged into two contrasting cycles: the productive and destructive cycles. That may sound complicated at first, but once you grasp the logic behind each cycle, it will be easy to remember.

FAR RIGHT Cats love trees and will often sit in them (although it is difficult for them to climb down). If your cat has no access to trees, she will probably favor your wooden furniture instead.

BELOW In feng shui terms, wood and water are closely linked in the productive cycle.

NOURISHING ENRICHMENT AREAS

According to the concept of the productive cycle, fire creates earth, earth is used in manufacturing metal, metal liquefies into water, water nourishes wood, and wood produces fire.

In the destructive cycle, fire melts metal, metal (as in axes) chops down wood, wood exhausts the earth by taking the goodness out of it, earth soaks up water, and water extinguishes fire.

As you will see in the following pages, the relationships between the elements will determine which remedies you choose for each enrichment area. Basically, you should use remedies connected with the elements that nourish the enrichment concerned, or at least reinforce it. However, you should avoid the elements that would destroy the one associated with that particular enrichment area.

THE ELEMENTAL CAT

Cats are generally associated with the wood element. Consequently, they prefer houses where the front door faces the directions associated with the wood element, east and southeast. But they are also attracted to houses facing north, the direction of the water element, because water nourishes wood. To maximize your cat's health and happiness, you should also ensure that her bedding is in either a single shade or a combination of colors which relate to the wood (green/brown) and/or water (black/blue) elements.

Once you've grasped the concept of the productive and destructive cycle and the way in which the elements relate to the various enrichment areas, you are ready to consider some common remedies which can be used to enhance the chi of the individual aspirations and generally enhance the quality of your life.

the pa kua

The pa kua (or bagua) is an octagonal device that is divided up into eight sections along the eight points of the compass. It is often depicted with the universal yin-yang symbol at its center. Each of the directions of the compass and complementary sections of the pa kua relates to one of the enrichment areas of your life (*see p. 78*).

FAR LEFT **A** cat curled in a corner, instinctively trying to shape the room into a more auspicious octagon by blocking off the corners.

LEFT A mirror set in an octagonal frame can be a very powerful tool.

THE SECTIONS OF THE PA KUA

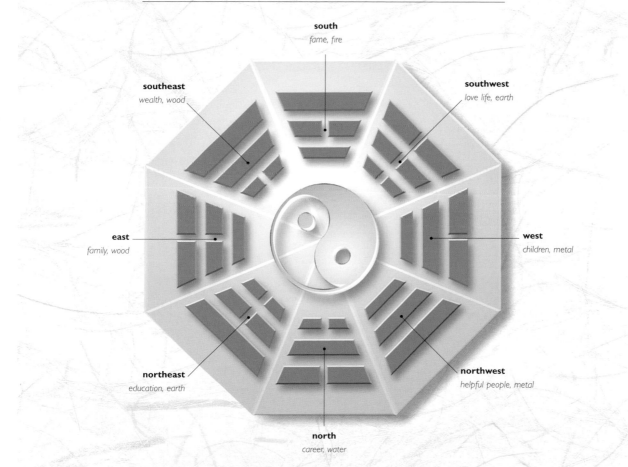

south
fame, fire

southeast
wealth, wood

southwest
love life, earth

east
family, wood

west
children, metal

northeast
education, earth

northwest
helpful people, metal

north
career, water

Each section of the pa kua contains a trigram from the *I Ching*. Trigrams are symbols that Fu Hsi, the legendary first emperor of China, is said to have discovered in the markings on the back of a tortoise he found on a riverbank. These trigrams can help you work out how the different directions within your home relate to the people who live with you. However, for this book's purposes, we shall simply look at how the pa kua can help you identify the different aspirational areas within your home.

85

using the pa kua

The beauty of the pa kua as employed in basic Compass School feng shui is that it can be applied to any type of dwelling, whether it be a studio apartment or a four-story mansion. In the former, it would apply to the apartment as a whole, but in the latter it would be used on each floor of the house. It can also be used in individual rooms or in the garden.

ABOVE **Draw up your house plan; remember that in feng shui, north is always at the bottom of a diagram and south is always at the top.**

GETTING STARTED

The pa kua is very easy to use. All you need to get started is a ruler, a compass, a pencil, and some paper, preferably both squared graph paper and tracing paper.

First, hold the compass leveled against the walls of your house to determine in which direction the house faces. Feng shui consultants use a specialized and very complicated-looking compass known as a Lo Pan, which you will often see on sale in Chinese shops, but this is a tool for experts. For your purposes, any simple but accurate compass will do. (But do make sure that you use a compass—guesswork can lead you horribly astray!)

Next, draw a floor plan of each story of your home on your squared paper, with south at the top of the page and north at the bottom.

Remember to include any extensions to the main structure, such as conservatories, built-in garages, and so on. Try to get the proportions of the rooms as accurate as possible.

Once you're sure you've got the plan right, copy the pa kua from the previous page onto the tracing paper, once again remembering to put the south at the top, and overlay it on top of your floor plan. You will then be able to see where each enrichment area falls within your home and you can begin to plan changes.

As you do this exercise, you may discover that, because your house is an "irregular" shape, or individual rooms do not form perfect squares or rectangles, some enrichment areas appear to be missing. This is a common situation and we will be telling you how to "replace" these areas later on in the book.

Think about which parts of your house your cat likes to settle in and how they relate to the enrichments. If she likes to sit in the southwest, is she detecting that you're having problems finding the right partner? Is she trying to help you over a rocky patch in your career by sleeping in the north? On the following pages, we'll tell you how you can harness her assistance and practice some self-help of your own to alleviate problems.

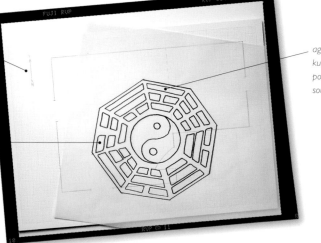

house plan with south positioned at the top

tracing paper showing pa kua laid on top of the house plan

again, the pa kua should be positioned with south at the top

LEFT **Lay the pa kua over your house plan. This will establish which parts of your house inhabit which enrichment areas.**

RIGHT **Trust your cat's instincts. If she habitually settles in one spot, check which enrichment area it lies in and have a look at that part of your life.**

common remedies

We've already talked about some of the common structural remedies in Part 2. Now we will look at the remedies that are usually applied specifically to the enrichment areas. They can be grouped into the categories listed on the right.

BELOW LEFT Enrichment areas respond to energizing remedies. The list below outlines the broad categories of remedies.

1 Light Either direct light sources, such as candles and lamps, or means of reflecting light, such as mirrors, crystals, and shiny objects.

2 Living things Plants, and pets such as dogs, goldfish, birds—and, of course, your cat!

3 Sound Wind chimes and bells.

4 Heavy objects Large stones or ornaments.

5 Moving objects Mobiles and banners.

6 Mechanical devices Television sets, radios, stereos, and other pieces of household electrical equipment.

7 Color Bright colors can be used to stir up chi; more muted shades will help to soothe it.

8 Symbols These are objects that the Chinese associate with luck, or that have significance for you.

A number of remedies can fall into more than one category. For example, wind chimes are both sound and movement remedies, and goldfish are both living things and a movement remedy (and the bubbling sound the water in an aquarium makes can provide a soothing sound remedy!).

CATS AS REMEDIES

Don't forget that your cat is a remedy in herself. All pets bring a yang element into the home, and with your cat's sensitivity to energies, she is particularly well equipped to detect where levels need to be corrected. You may find she favors the family, wealth, and career enrichments, as they lie in her own most fortunate directions—but, after all, those are not bad areas to start with!

You could try enticing your cat to settle into other enrichment areas that you feel need to be enlivened, but she may have her own agenda. If you want her to move into the love enrichment, but she stubbornly keeps settling in the career aspiration, could it be that you are devoting too much time to your romantic life, when you should be concentrating more on your job? If she really doesn't want to know about a particular enrichment area, perhaps it's because she perceives a greater need elsewhere.

If you get really desperate for her help and she still won't cooperate, remember that, in the absence of the real thing, the ancient Chinese would put up pictures of cats in their corn stores. A photograph of your cat in an enrichment corner could provide just the amount of energy you need to turn things around.

FAR LEFT Although this cat is probably attracted by the bird's snack potential, in other circumstances pets can work together to form effective remedies.

wealth

This enrichment is associated with the wood element, and so is your cat, so hopefully you won't have any problems persuading her to frequent these areas—which should be to your mutual benefit!

ABOVE Fish, particularly goldfish, are traditionally thought to attract wealth. If you cannot have the real thing, ornaments or pictures—"virtual fish"— can be just as successful.

CREATING MOVEMENT

If you do feel that your cat needs some encouragement, one of the most traditional Chinese remedies for increasing your wealth is installing a fish tank. Just look at how many Chinese restaurants have them! You'll also notice that they usually contain an odd number of occupants, generally nine, and that although they are goldfish, one of them is black. Goldfish are considered beneficial in generating wealth, as is keeping an odd number (especially nine). The black fish is protection against burglary.

But a fish tank might not be the ideal solution for your home. Remember that living creatures can only be effective remedies if they are healthy and happy; otherwise, they could have the opposite effect. And bear in mind that there isn't a cat living on this earth who doesn't like a fish dinner! Although you may be able to weight down the top of the tank to stop inquisitive paws from reaching in, your cat is still going to be fascinated by the movement of the fish. As a safer alternative, you could put a collection of fish ornaments in this corner.

RIGHT Movement in the wealth sector is believed to stir up sluggish finances, so consider hanging a mobile in this area. Make it a fish mobile, to double your chances and also to entertain your cat.

Incidentally, many feng shui consultants strongly oppose installing a fish tank in the bedroom, even if this is where your wealth enrichment lies and your cat is banned from this room. A fish tank is too potent a remedy, they say, and can be very hazardous to your health in a room devoted to rest and regeneration.

▌ BATHROOMS AND KITCHENS

If your wealth enrichment is in the vicinity of your kitchen, you're in luck! That is a good omen that you will never be short of money. If it lies in your bathroom, though, it's not such good news. It means that money is going to leak away from you at every opportunity. So fix leaking faucets and pipes immediately, keep plugs in the sink, and don't forget to lower the toilet lid after use. (Don't despair—my wealth area is in the bathroom too!)

Movement is said to be good for stirring up finances, so why not hang a mobile in this area? You can also try putting a child's pinwheel where it can catch the breeze. Once your cat sees it move, this simple toy is likely to provide her with hours of enjoyment and persuade her to spend more time in the wealth enrichment.

ABOVE **It seems that cats have always been fascinated by fish: whether it is the bright movement, the watery environment, the energy generated, or the prospect of a tasty dinner that attracts them, has not been established. If you do keep a real fish tank, make sure its inhabitants are well-protected from your cat's investigative paw.**

career

The career enrichment lies in another of your cat's favorite directions—the north—so this should also be an area that she doesn't need much persuasion to settle in.

RUNNING WATER

Water is associated with this direction, so if you feel that your career has stalled, you can start things moving by putting a water feature in this corner. Indoor fountains and other water features, such as miniature ponds, can now be purchased quite easily and make an attractively different focal point in the room—and your cat will probably find it fascinating to watch!

Make sure that you keep the water fresh and clean, because this will reflect on your career prospects. If your cat tries to drink the water, it could be a sign that you are working too hard and she is trying to protect your health by slowing your career down.

OTHER IDEAS

If you don't like the idea of a water feature in your room—and some sensitive people do find that the sound of running water makes them continually want to go to the bathroom!—try hanging a picture of moving water in this enrichment area instead. Look for a picture of a waterfall, or perhaps an attractive landscape with a rushing river in the foreground.

Movement is also thought to be a good remedy for a career that seems to be stagnating, so hang a wind chime or a mobile in this corner. If these can feature the color blue, so much the better, since blue is the color associated with this enrichment.

Even burning incense may help, as the smoke curling upward will be another source of action. And make sure that this corner is kept very neat, because any clutter could also symbolize obstacles in your career path.

If you have specific career problems that you want to put right, use your imagination and employ a bit of symbolism. Think about your goals and try to find something that will represent them symbolically to put in this enrichment area. For example, if you would like to travel more with your work, place a globe in this space. If you're not sure which direction to pursue in your career, spread out a map in this corner. Every time you look at your chosen symbolic object, it will reinforce your ambitions in your mind.

ABOVE **If it is impractical to put a water feature in your career corner, choose a picture which represents water, such as a river or waterfall, instead.**

FAR LEFT **If your office is at home, you will be familiar with the popular feline trick of sitting on your papers as you work. However, your cat's presence in your career corner will help to bring you success.**

LEFT **Symbolic objects can stimulate energy: place a globe in your career space to combine work and travel.**

93

love life

If you want to improve your love life, it's best to concentrate the enrichments in the southwest corner of a room you spend a lot of time in, such as your living room or study. Bedrooms should not be overloaded with enrichments, because they will disrupt your sleep; bathrooms are too inauspicious and kitchens are too busy. If your living room or study is in the southwest part of your home, so much the better.

ABOVE Crystals focus the earth element in the southwest corner of love and relationships. Choose two crystals to place there, preferably red or at least pink ones such as rose quartz, known in the West as the "love crystal."

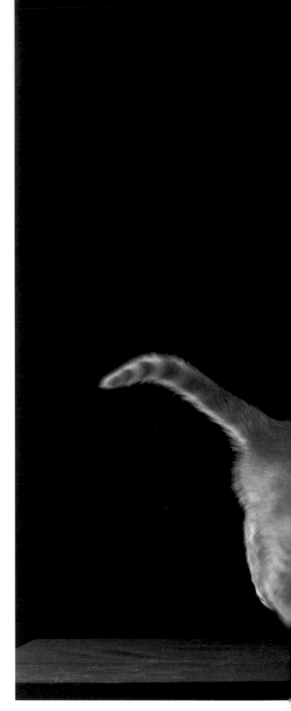

THINK IN PAIRS

Single people looking for the love of their life should think in pairs as far as enhancements for the love aspiration are concerned. It's often been noted by feng shui practitioners that single people tend to favor pictures featuring a single figure—and often a sad-looking figure at that! Instead, find pictures of happy couples for the southwest corner of your room. If you have a pair of cats, a picture of them looking contented in each other's company will do just as well. The important focal points here are couples and happiness for good feng shui.

A pair of lovebirds are also thought to be a good enhancement to this area, but, for the same reason that you should think carefully about installing a fish tank, this is definitely a no-no in a household that includes a cat! However, once again, a picture will do just as well.

CRYSTALS AND COLORS

The southwest is governed by the earth element, so crystals will also have a potent effect in this corner. Because fire produces earth, candles are also a good idea—just remember to have a pair of them. (Never leave your cat alone in a room with lit candles—she could knock them over or accidentally burn herself as she passes the flames.)

According to Chinese tradition, the peony flower and the color red are both thought to have auspicious associations with love—in fact, it is quite common for Chinese brides to get married in red outfits. So a painting of a peony and a splash of scarlet paint or fabric may also be effective in this corner.

If you already have a partner, but feel the sparkle has gone out of your love life, dig out some photographs of the happiest times of your life together and put them in this corner. Find some mementos of times when your relationship was really good and move them to this enrichment area to revive the good times.

Incidentally, some practitioners believe that if your cat spends too much time here, you may have a great relationship with her—to the exclusion of a partner! If this is the case it might be wise to discourage her.

ABOVE **The path of true love rarely runs smoothly. It may be time for these cats to rekindle the energy in their love corner.**

LEFT **Affectionate cats will bring a great advantage to your southwest corner, if you can persuade them to spend some time there.**

95

helpful people

The term "helpful people" is an ancient feng shui concept which encompasses everyone who is supportive of you and helps you to function at your best, from your cleaning person to your boss (assuming that your boss is supportive!).

GOLD AND SILVER

The element relating to the 'helpful people' corner is metal. Metal remedies tend to have a stabilizing effect, and provide support that you can rely on. Metallic colors include silver and gold, and it can be especially beneficial to put ornaments made of these metals in the northwest section of your home.

Wind chimes can be very potent remedies for this enrichment, provided they are made of metal and not bamboo or ceramic. They should also have hollow rods rather than solid ones, which will enable them to channel chi upward.

If you feel that you need more helpful people in your life, energize this area with table lamps made from metal or with a metallic finish, and try to combine earth and metal remedies. (Earth produces metal, remember.) One way of doing this is to have plants in metallic bowls.

Put photographs of people who are or have been particularly helpful to you in this area, preferably in metal frames. If you have pictures that symbolize the kind of help you may need in the future, put those here too.

If this area falls in your bathroom, hang a large wind chime from the ceiling to "suppress" the bad luck and keep it from stopping helpful people from entering your life.

DO SOME GOOD

Some feng shui practitioners suggest that the helpful people enrichment is very much a two-way concept. This enrichment area is connected with charity, and they believe that if you try hard to help others—for example, with voluntary work—your actions will in turn attract more helpful people into your life.

It's debatable whether your cat can help you in this particular enrichment. As a creature belonging to the wood element, she will probably feel uncomfortable in the metal element and refuse to settle there—and it would be cruel to try to force her.

ABOVE **A combination of metal and earth will help to energize the area associated with helpful people. For instance, try putting your pot plants into decorative metal bowls.**

LEFT **Cats could be classed as "helpful people" in themselves. They seem to understand the two-way traffic involved; they offer companionship, physical contact, and affection in return for food and shelter.**

FAR LEFT **Your cat may not feel comfortable in the area governed by the metal element. Do not force her to stay there.**

education

The education enrichment does not just affect the kind of studying and learning you do in school or college—its influence extends to self-development of any kind, from playing a musical instrument to working on your computer.

ABOVE Cats enjoy the chi generated by electricity, and love to sit on electric keyboards—particularly if you are trying to use them.

RIGHT Your cat's proverbial curiosity may also lead her to explore the education space in your home, helping to stir up positive chi there.

▍ POSITIVE EFFECTS

This enrichment is situated in the northeast corner, and if you can locate your study or work room in this area, it should have a very positive effect on your efforts. If your home isn't big enough for you to have a separate study, put your desk in the northeast corner of your living room. This is obviously a good place to keep your computer or anything else you need to help you to improve yourself, such as textbooks or application forms for jobs.

As usual, the bathroom is not an auspicious area for your education enrichment to fall in, but if this is the case, put a large stone on top of your toilet to stabilize chi and prevent the results of your hard work being "flushed away!" Don't use any wood remedies in your education area, because wood destroys earth and will demolish your hopes of success.

▍ A KIND OF ELECTRICITY

It's funny how your cat always wants to sit on your lap or the keyboard when you are working at the computer! This is because she is excited by the amount of chi it produces. In fact, any kind of electrical equipment will have a stimulating effect on this area—but remember that these appliances can sometimes be too powerful, so you must be careful not to overload the enrichment with them.

Another word of warning: you should not hang a mirror where it can reflect this area. This will only double the amount of work you have to do to improve yourself!

Crystals are said to be an extremely potent feng shui enhancement for academic success. Natural quartz and rock crystals are particularly recommended as the most energizing crystals. With the increased interest in New Age religion, and the simple fact that more people have become aware of the beauty of crystals, they are easy to find these days. Choose one that really appeals to you, or use one that has been given to you by a close friend. Keep your crystal in top condition by cleaning it at regular intervals—wash it in sea water or mineral water, and dry it thoroughly afterward. (Washing it in tap water will reduce its effectiveness.) If you're taking an exam, having a solid crystal ball in the northeast corner of your bedroom is said to bring good luck.

BELOW A solid crystal ball placed in the education corner will give you an extra boost at exam time.

keep your crystal ball clear and bright by cleaning it often with a soft cloth

wash your crystals in mineral water or—even better— sea water

fame

The fame enrichment should be handled with care. It is associated with the fire element, which, while it can be the source of inspiration and passion, can also be unpredictable and dangerous. No wonder so many celebrities seem to have problems handling their newfound fame!

BELOW This cat is sitting quietly in front of an auspicious red backdrop, working to improve the fame enrichment area

FIRE AND LIGHT

This area also overlaps with your career aspirations, so if you have problems getting ahead at work, you should pay attention to this enrichment as well. Put a picture in the south corner that represents something you are working toward. It will energize your efforts and help you to reach your goals.

It is not always possible to have an open fire in your home, but if you do have one and it happens to be in the south direction, then this can be very good feng shui. An artificial fire with jet flames is equally effective.

Naked flames, such as candles or oil burners, strong (but not glaring) lighting, mirrors to reflect available illumination, and the color red can all prove beneficial here. Introduce each remedy individually and then note its effect. You need to be careful not to overdo things. Too little fire may leave you feeling uninspired, but too much can result in the destruction of your plans. An excess of fire can also cause disagreements between the people living in the house.

ARTISTIC INSPIRATION

Less inflammatory remedies are objects that have either been created through inspiration or can inspire others, such as a piece of beautiful sculpture, a painting by an old master, or CDs of classical music.

Then, of course, there's always your cat. She is a wood animal, and wood produces fire, so see if she will make her bed in the south direction. If she refuses to sleep there, once again simply placing her photograph in that corner will be just as effective.

LEFT Wood fuels the fire of fame. Encourage your cat to spend time in the south corner if you want to boost your chances of celebrity.

RIGHT Candles, incense, and the color red can all enhance your fame corner. Fire is a powerful element, so do not overuse it.

a red lamp will create a warming glow in your fame enrichment

create fire with a candle—but ensure that it is well-shielded from your cat

incense will not only stimulate your fame corner, it will also perfume your house

family

Your cat will probably enjoy sleeping in your family enrichment, because, like her, it is governed by the wood element. Situated in the east, this is the corner where you should display family photographs, the ones in which you are all enjoying yourselves, happy in each other's company. This will help to maintain harmony within the family group. (If the pictures include your cat, so much the better—it will also benefit relations between her and the rest of the family.)

ABOVE **Choose round-leaved plants to encourage good family relationships. Spiky leaves are thought to inspire disharmony.**

▍ GREEN, GROWING THINGS

Another way to energize relationships within the family is to place plants here or display pictures of vegetation. Plants that hold water in their leaves, such as succulents, are particularly beneficial in this area, as they also contain a water remedy. However, any plants used as a remedy should have rounded leaves, so avoid cacti. According to feng shui precepts, cacti and other plants with spiky leaves have no place within the home. When put in the family enrichment, these plants can cause arguments and discord. Also avoid any plants that are poisonous to cats, but perhaps grow some catnip as a special treat.

RIGHT **Cut flowers are not thought to be a good remedy, as they are considered to be dying. This cat is demonstrating a particularly ruthless approach to the problem.**

THE FENG SHUI OF FLOWERS

Some feng shui practitioners frown on using vases of fresh flowers as a remedy, on the grounds that, as they have been deprived of their roots, they are dying as soon as you cut them. However, it seems hard to ban cut flowers from the home, especially since in a vase they have the added strength of a water remedy. If you do decide to use them, keep the water fresh and clear and throw individual blooms away as soon as they start to fade.

If your cat starts to chew on a plant or flower arrangement, she may just like the taste. But if she often seems intent on destroying plants and flowers you've brought home, it could be because she feels overloaded with the amount of energy they bring with them.

If you can't have fresh flowers in your home—if, for example, you're allergic—feng shui experts say silk flowers are a good substitute. But plastic flowers are not—man-made materials like plastic are bad feng shui!

ABOVE Growing plants provide abundant energy and resonate well with the family corner, which is associated with the wood element. If you have no plants in the home, your cat will seek them outside.

children

Like your cat, children are a great source of yang energy,
because if a child is happy and healthy, he or she will always
be surrounded by love, sound, and activity. So if music blares
from your child's bedroom for hours on end, relax—things are
just as they should be! If you don't have any children, this
enrichment, which lies in the west, may represent a pet
project, a special hobby, or that novel you always meant to
write—something that you are personally creating or that's
"your baby." If this area becomes cluttered, your creativity may
become blocked, and women may find it difficult to conceive.

LEFT Kittens are full of yang
energy, just like all young
beings, children included.
Including a kitten in a family
will amplify the positive
energy in the home.

COLOR YOUR CHILD'S WORLD

Color is a potent remedy in the children's
enrichment. To maintain your children's energy,
keep this area—and the children's own
bedrooms—painted in bright colors. Colors
from the warm end of the spectrum are especially energizing. The children's enrichment is
governed by the metal element, which is usually
represented by a circle, so it's good to have lots
of curves in this area—if your "baby" is a special
project, curved lines and surfaces will help you
to bring it to fruition. Earth is another good
remedy to use in this area, so placing plants in
metal bowls here may be useful. Don't put
plants in your child's room, though, as they will
disrupt his or her sleep.

Your cat may find it uncomfortable in this
area, as she belongs to the wood element, but
she may sneak in when the children are away
to calm the flow of chi.

CREATIVE CHAOS

If you've cleared all the clutter out of the rest
of your house, but despair of ever being able to
create good feng shui within your home when
you see the mess of your teenager's bedroom,
don't let this be the source of family arguments.
Teenagers are young adults and are entitled to
do what they like within their own personal
space. To prevent the disorder from affecting

the rest of the house, keep the door to the
room firmly closed and note which enrichment
area of the home it falls in. If, for example, it is
in the career enrichment and you are worried
about the effect of the untidiness on your
career, simply place a remedy in the career
corner of your own bedroom to counteract any
possible detrimental fallout. And just remember
that the energy that is generated by your
teenager's loud music and their constant stream
of visiting friends may actually be acting as a
stimulant to your career!

BELOW Your kitten will
adapt her energy patterns
to synchronize with your
child's so that their joint
energies will not conflict.

missing corners

RIGHT The cat who perches for hours in a sunny spot may be covering a missing corner that she has discovered in your garden.

If you live in an irregularly shaped house, you will probably find that it has "missing corners." That is, if you square off your floor plan, there are some areas of the pa kua that simply do not exist in your home, so that one or more enrichment areas appears to be missing from it.

RIGHT A missing corner can be disguised with a strategically placed mirror or plant. Your cat will often spend some part of her day sitting there.

PUTTING BACK WHAT'S MISSING

Don't worry. The fact that your wealth enrichment is missing doesn't mean that you will always be broke, and if your love enrichment does not exist, it doesn't mean you'll never find the love of your life. There are some remedies that have been developed specifically to compensate for missing corners.

The important thing is to create the impression that the corner is not really "missing" at all. For example, hanging a mirror on each side of the "corner" will give the optical impression that it's actually there. Alternatively, you can put a light outside in the missing corner and shine it toward the house. If the missing corner is in the garden, you may find that your cat will be happy to sit there when she is outdoors.

There are also a number of specific remedies which may be employed to deal with individual missing enrichments.

WEALTH Dangle a crystal along the edge of the missing corner, or hang two wind chimes there, one on either side of it.

FAME Introduce the color red or orange with ornaments or furnishings along the sides of the missing corner, or place a flame-related painting on the wall.

FAMILY Arrange flowers or plants around the missing corner.

CAREER Place a water feature against the wall and add touches of blue and black.

Finally, when you were overlaying your floor plan with the pa kua, you may have noticed that there is a circle at the center of it (often filled by the yin-yang symbol). This has an importance all its own. It identifies the heart of your home, the focal point of yin and yang, which should ideally fall in the dining room or living room. This area should be kept particularly clear and tidy. Chi emanating from this area affects the rest of the home, and so this space should be full of movement, happiness, and sociability. If it is an area that you don't use very much, like a storeroom, see if you can make some changes to convert it into a place where you and your family will spend more time.

beginning to experiment

Now that you've learned the basic principles of Compass School feng shui, you can start trying out some remedies of your own. The most important thing to remember is that there are no hard and fast rules—experiment with the remedies, using your imagination and intuition, until you find out what works for you. Be flexible in your approach, and don't expect instant results with the first thing you try.

WORKING WITH YOUR CAT

Always remember to work alongside your cat to achieve balanced, healthy levels of chi. It's important, though, not to view your cat as a chi-converting machine—don't rely on her to bring peace and harmony to your home all by herself. She has her own needs, just as you do, and you should respect them. If you continually move her bed from one enrichment area to another, she will only become unsettled and unhappy and will not work for your benefit.

Your cat also has her own instincts, which are more finely tuned to chi energy than yours are. If she insists on settling in a particular spot, it may be because she is instinctively aware of what you need—which may be different from what you think you need.

Watch your cat closely to see how she reacts to individual remedies. If she starts chewing at a plant or pulling down a wind chime, she may feel they're an inappropriate solution, or too strong. Try replacing them with something she finds easier to live with.

LESS IS MORE

A common mistake made by many people when they first start to work with feng shui is trying to cram as many remedies as possible into the various enrichment areas. This is counter-productive. In feng shui, "more" does not mean "better." In fact, the reverse applies—a surplus of remedies may create more problems than it solves. After all, why clear out your home only to clutter it up again with too many mirrors, mobiles, and ornaments?

All the conflicting energies flying around the house will soon make your cat stressed and agitated. She may feel the need to move on to a more tranquil environment, where she can do her work in peace. Introduce one remedy at a time, and take time to observe its effects on your life and on your cat's behavior before you make any further changes.

LEFT Although your cat is an invaluable feng shui tool, allow her to indulge in some more traditional feline pursuits as well.

BELOW Avoid overloading your house—and your cat —with remedies. In feng shui terms too much is as harmful as too little.

fine-tuning

Once you feel you have the right remedies in place, there may still be some fine-tuning to be done. There is a very wise old saying: Be careful what you wish for because you might get it! Sometimes when you want something very badly, it's easy to get carried away and introduce remedies appropriate to an enrichment area, but so powerful that they backfire on you.

RIGHT Let your cat be your balance-monitor. If remedies need to be replaced, her behavior will probably let you know.

BELOW A new kitten may be adorable but will bring extra yang energy into your home and you may need to tone down some of the remedies previously used.

FINDING THE BALANCE

A friend of mine, working on a tip from feng shui practitioner Lillian Too, activated her romance area with a picture of a pair of wild horses, said to be a very potent remedy for enhancing your love life. She then added a pair of large red candles to enhance the effect further. She ended up in the throes of a stormy affair, which, while passionate and exhilarating, was also very troublesome and severely exhausting.

Like the wild horses, the wild romance was simply too much for my friend to control and eventually came to a fairly devastating end. She consequently replaced the tall candles with small, night-light type candles. She removed the horse picture and put in its place a photograph of a couple holding hands and smiling at each other. She eventually ended up in a calmer, but equally loving, relationship, with a boyfriend who is now also her best friend.

CHANGE FOR THE BETTER

Bear in mind that you will also need to change remedies from time to time, as your personal circumstances and opportunities change. Suppose, for example, you bought a new kitten. With all the added yang energy she would inevitably bring to your household, you would probably need to tone down the remedies that you'd been using in order to accommodate the influx of chi into the home.

It is also possible for remedies to lose their potency after they've been in place for a while. In my experience, they almost seem to "fade" visually as they become exhausted and need to be replaced by something else.

So have fun experimenting, use the remedies judiciously, and keep an eye on your cat's reactions to see whether you are going right or wrong. And remember: balance is the key word when you are working with feng shui.

4

a cat's garden

form school

The Form School of feng shui was mentioned earlier, in Part 2 (*see p. 54*). It is the oldest school of feng shui and is not as concerned with the effects the points of the compass have on your home, and consequently your life, as with how the features inherent in your home's location have a bearing on it. Form School is therefore important to the garden, because this is what surrounds many modern-day homes.

The first step in Form School feng shui is to examine the environment in which your home is placed. According to Form School practitioners, the best location for your home is a dwelling that faces south. Ideally, the house should be surrounded on all four sides by hills, known as the "four celestial animals," as they have been given symbolic animal names. At the back should be the tallest hills of all, those governed by the "tortoise." In the east, there should be the slightly smaller hills of the "dragon" and to the west, the hills of the "tiger," which should be lower still. In front of the house should be the smallest hill of all—in fact, not

actually much more than a small mound—belonging to the "phoenix." This perfect environment is completed by a river which runs around the front of the site.

Feng shui practitioners often compare the ideal configuration of hills to an armchair, supporting the house on three sides, while the phoenix acts as a footrest. (Please note that, even if your home doesn't face south, the tortoise is always sited at the back of your house, the dragon to the left as you look out of your front door, the tiger to the right, and the phoenix in the front.)

THE CHARACTERISTICS OF THE CELESTIAL ANIMALS

The tortoise is believed to be slow and kindly, and nurtures the occupants of the home. The dragon, like all dragons in Chinese folklore, is a very wise and auspicious creature, and offers protection and good luck. The tiger is powerful, but also unpredictable, and so should be handled with great care. It will fiercely protect the occupants of the house, but it can also turn against them. The phoenix is an optimistic creature, which can survive even death. It brings luck and fame.

If you live in a town or in a particularly flat part of the countryside, the concept of the four celestial animals can still apply. Look at the man-made features which surround your home and in your mind's eye, use these as symbolic replacements for the hills. The building at the rear of your home takes the place of the tortoise, that to the left the dragon, and so on. Similarly, if you live in an isolated spot, other surrounding features, such as trees, banks, or barns, can be substitutes for hills.

BELOW According to the Form School of feng shui, your home is guarded by four animals: the tortoise, the dragon, the tiger, and the phoenix, each of which are stationed at a different compass point.

the tortoise nurtures the house's accupants

the tiger is protective but unpredictable

the phoenix brings luck and fame

the dragon is very auspicious

RIGHT Your cat may be a small and distant relation of the mighty tiger, but she can be a powerful feng shui force in your home.

activating the four celestial animals

Wherever you live and whatever you use to help you to represent the four celestial animals, you may find that their proportions are not ideal. There are remedies you can use to help correct them; for example, you can plant trees or shrubs to represent the different animals.

TORTOISE

Keeping a live tortoise in your backyard will symbolize the presence of the Form School tortoise. Tortoises are relatively unde-manding pets and they come

with their own armor, into which they can withdraw when your cat becomes too curious, so the pair should be able to live alongside each other peaceably! However, since the cruel import trade in tortoises was justifiably banned, they have become harder to obtain and more expensive to buy. Bear in mind that during the cold months of winter, you will either have to bring your tortoise inside the house or prepare a snug box in which it can hibernate in an outbuilding. If you don't feel you want to shoulder the added responsibility of another pet, a ceramic or bronze representation of a tortoise, when placed in your backyard, will provide a satisfactory substitute.

TIGER

The notori-
ous strength
of the tiger
must be kept
firmly under control; otherwise, his power will overwhelm the occupants of the home, which in turn may bring them bad luck. On the other hand, if he is too small, their life will be uneventful and boring. The best way to adjust the size

of the tiger is to grow low shrubs on this side of the house. If tall trees are cultivated here, they will allow the tiger to dominate the dragon, and the tiger may then turn his aggression on the occupants of the house.

DRAGON

Planting trees on the dragon's side of the house is the most effective way to adjust his proportions. However, bear in mind how big the trees will grow in maturity and don't place them too

close to the house where they may block off light to the windows, as this will make the house too yin.

PHOENIX

Probably the easiest of the four celestial animals to replace is the phoenix. In order to activate this area, you can try building a small rock

garden; or you can
make sure that the
front of your yard is
encircled by a low
brick wall. Other
simple remedies are
to either dig a mound
in the front yard,
or simply place a
large rock there in
order to symbolize
the missing phoenix.

FAR LEFT **Your cat can detect imbalance in the garden or yard around your house as well as she can inside it.**

creating a sanctuary

Feng shui is as important in the garden, yard, or property around your home as it is indoors. Documents relating to the feng shui of gardens have existed for over 3,000 years. Don't worry; you are not about to learn a new set of rules and concepts. The same simple principles of feng shui apply, whether they are being employed inside or outside the house.

RIGHT Your cat will seek out the areas that need fine-tuning in your garden and will spend some time there absorbing or generating energy.

BELOW Observe your cat's behavior in the garden as you do in your house: her body language will let you know if there is any imbalance outside.

When you use feng shui in the garden, you are still looking to achieve balance between yin and yang and to facilitate and freshen the flow of chi. And in a similar way to that in which your cat helps you indoors, she can do the same in the garden, in signaling which areas of your life need to be enriched and also in identifying areas of potentially harmful geopathic stress.

Once again, you should endeavor to keep your garden, like your house, clean and neat. Paths and lawns should be swept regularly, and dead or dying plants removed swiftly, but don't go overboard. Employing feng shui in the garden does not mean laying paths in strict straight lines, keeping plants in squared-off beds, savagely pruning trees and shrubs, and maintaining the lawn in such a ruthlessly manicured state that people are frightened to step onto it. Plants and trees should be allowed to grow as naturally as possible—or at least, they should give that visual impression.

TIME OUT

Some people spend more time working in their yard than actually sitting back and appreciating it. This is not the Chinese way of doing things! Of course, gardening, although ultimately rewarding, can be very hard work, but equally, you should make time to enjoy the fruit of your labors, as your cat does!

Your garden should be a place for enjoyment and relaxation for both you and your cat. You should be able to sit out in it and talk with friends, read a book, eat al fresco, or simply appreciate nature and absorb its peaceful energy. Equally, there should be areas of the garden where your cat can have fun sharpening her claws on trees, stalking in the bushes, or scratching around in her own area of earth without upsetting your handiwork. You should both be able to rest and recuperate in your garden—and while she is doing so, your cat can also be helping to improve its feng shui.

a cat's garden

When you are planning your garden, remember to take your cat's needs into account as well. Cats love being outside and are instinctively in tune with nature. Look at the way in which, when your cat is slightly off-color, she instinctively chews on the kinds of grasses that will act as medicine to make her feel better.

Vets confirm that eating grass is good for a cat's digestive system and may even help her to obtain extra vitamins that she is not getting elsewhere. Even cats that are kept indoors at all times should have access to a patch of grass, albeit grown in a bowl, so make sure that there is at least a pocket handkerchief-sized lawn for the benefit of your outdoor cat.

Of course, cats always enjoy basking in the sun—especially when they have a dry stone foundation on which to lie. Old cats, in particular, love the way in which stone retains the heat of the sun and reflects it back, warming their aching joints and allowing them to soak up its energy. Any cat will enjoy lying on the stone surround of a garden pond, idly watching the movement of the water, or stretching out asleep in a rock garden.

FELINE FEATURES

Rock gardens are, in fact, very much a part of traditional Chinese gardens and something which you should seriously consider incorporating in your yard, not only for your cat's benefit, but also for your own. The stability of a rock garden balances out the movement of water, and they are said to help prevent health or wealth from slipping away from the household.

If you are digging out a pond, you can use the leftover soil to create your rock garden and site it in one of the enrichment areas associated with earth, i.e., northwest or southwest. Use rounded stones, avoiding rocks with sharp edges or threatening shapes. Copy the ancient Chinese and try to incorporate a wood

element in it as well, such as a small piece of driftwood or an old branch that has assumed an interesting shape. As a wood creature, your cat will appreciate this addition.

It will also be to both your advantages if you plant yourself an herb garden. Incorporate sweet-smelling herbs, which will improve the chi circulating within the garden, and don't forget to make some additions that your cat will enjoy. Catnip, also know as catmint, and valerian will send her into an almost trance-like state of ecstasy, as well as being good for chi. And if you construct your herb garden in an octagon-shaped flowerbed, it is considered most auspicious feng shui.

ABOVE **A rock garden of sun-baked stones will provide a comfortable sleeping spot.**

FAR LEFT **Include a patch of grass and if possible some catnip (*Nepeta cataria*) in the garden for your cat.**

BELOW **A feng shui master takes some time out.**

structure

Constructing a feng shui garden doesn't necessarily mean that your yard will end up looking like the illustration on a willow pattern plate! Western-style gardens can easily be adapted with the application of feng shui principles— although, of course, if you did want to recreate the attractive minimalism of a typically Chinese garden, it would be a very worthwhile and rewarding project.

FAR RIGHT **If your garden strikes the right balance, it will be a place where your cat will relax. Too much plant energy may encourage excessive hunting.**

For now, let's just take it down to feng shui basics. You should not be able to see the entire garden at a single glance; with no obstacles in its path to deflect it, chi will rush through and out of your garden. It should be able to meander down paths, curl around hidden arbors, and seek refreshment from water features and stability from rock gardens.

On the other hand, don't go overboard and cram plants, trees, shrubs, arboreal features, and garden furniture into every available space in your yard, because this will have just as adverse an effect as too much clutter in your home. Many practitioners define the perfect feng shui garden as one from which nothing else could be taken away without detracting from its attractiveness. Added to which, although your cat may enjoy hunting in jungle conditions, if your garden becomes a virtual killing field for birds and small mammals, their fear and subsequent death will generate very bad energy.

CIRCULATING CHI

Just as you do when you are indoors, use your eyes and your intuition to imagine how chi will circulate around the garden and how it will be affected by the obstacles it meets along the way. Use curving paths, flowerbeds, screens, and pergolas to direct its flow and make use of differing heights, through variably sized plants, bushes, and trees or specially constructed banks to regulate its speed. At all times, keep thinking of maintaining a balance, between water and rock, movement and stillness, sun and shadow, and so on throughout the garden.

Feng shui practitioners consider it favorable to incorporate something representing each of the five elements—water, metal, wood, fire, and earth—in the garden. Take a look back to *pp. 20–21* to remind yourself of their properties. Wood and earth are usually already there, but for water, you can add a pond or water feature. A statue or a sundial may be used for metal, and fire can be represented by a barbecue or even by red flowers. Also aim to incorporate two of the most important feng shui shapes—a circle and an octagon—in its design, perhaps in the form of a flowerbed or pond. And finally, if you're really planning to garden Chinese style, remember that they prefer to grow flowers in varying shades of white, reserving an occasional splash of color—particularly red—to provide a dramatic contrast.

RIGHT **Certain elements are needed to create a feng shui garden. The aim is to beguile chi energy with curves but not to block it with too many obstacles.**

shrubs can be used to block off corners

symbolic statues are potent cures

a winding path encourages chi to circulate through the entire garden

a rockery balances the volatility of the water feature

fish are always associated with good luck

plan a harmonious color scheme when bedding out plants

common remedies

Just as the use of the pa kua is the same whether indoors or out, the same common feng shui remedies that were used inside the house—such as light, sound, movement, color and so on—can also be adapted for use in the garden. For example, the sound of a fountain that refreshes chi will at the same time incorporate the water element and the movement remedy.

FAR LEFT Just as in the house, your cat's benign presence in any part of the garden will enhance the life area located there.

In the same way that indoor cures were related to the governing elements of each enrichment area, you should be thinking along the same lines when it comes to implementing remedies in the garden. Similarly, your cat is an enhancement in whatever enrichment area of the garden she chooses to settle.

WEALTH As this is associated with the wood element, this is an obvious place to site a water feature or pond. And even though you may not dare to keep an aquarium indoors where your cat is on the loose, the garden is one place where you can keep fish in relative safety—provided you take a few precautions. You can read more about this on *pp. 134–135*.

CAREER This is another area which will benefit from the addition of water. But this may not necessarily be a pond; it can even be a garden hose or sprinkler. Remember to keep this area in particular tidy and open, otherwise you may encounter obstacles at work.

LOVE LIFE This enrichment is a good place to site a love seat or arbor. Create an area where you and your partner can sit together and relax, simply enjoying each other's company—and the company of your cat, of course! A pair of statues here, representing a loving couple or perhaps a couple of love birds, will increase the stability of the relationship, the stone "grounding" it to the earth.

HELPFUL PEOPLE It is a good idea to encourage birds to congregate here as they are "helpful people" to gardeners—but first read *pp. 134–135*! A large boulder or a rock garden located here will create stability in this direction.

EDUCATION This area is a good place to site tables and chairs, particularly if you are planning to work out of doors. A ceramic tub full of plants can also be useful here.

FAME Keep bushes and trees in this area well-pruned, so that your achievements are not overshadowed, and keep it well-lit to enhance your reputation.

FAMILY As this area is governed by wood, it is a good place to situate wooden garden furniture—particularly chairs and tables where the whole family can gather together.

CHILDREN As this enrichment is governed by metal, it is the obvious place for children's toys such as swings, slides, and climbing frames.

Remember also the colors associated with each element within the pa kua, as listed on *pp. 80–81*, and use plants featuring the complementary shades—red flowers in the south, yellow in the northeast and southwest, and so on—to activate these areas.

ABOVE **Place stone furniture and a flower arbor in the love life** corner. Sit there often with your partner— your cat will soon join you.

the pa kua

When you are planning your feng shui garden, use the pa kua in just the same way that you would employ it in your house. Lay it over a plan of your yard and identify where all the different enrichment areas are situated. You should also mark on your plan potential hazards, such as missing corners in the shape of your garden and poison arrows, either within it or overlooking it. (If you have separate front and back yards, lay the pa kua over each individually.)

RIGHT Even a young cat has feng shui sense. If you find her sitting in what seems to be a dank or unproductive spot, she may have found an area of geopathic stress.

RIGHT Use your pa kua diagram to plan your garden. Place it over a plan of your garden to find out which parts of the garden represent the various areas of your life.

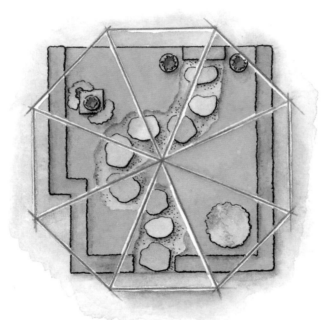

If there are awkward corners or sharp verticals which constitute poison arrows within the garden, soften them by encouraging climbing roses or creepers to grow over them. If your home is overlooked by a building which causes bad feng shui, such as a hospital, an area such as a cemetery, or a structure like a power pylon, grow tall trees or an evergreen hedge in front of it to blot out the sight of it and create a barrier between your home and this source of bad energy. If that is impossible, add some trellising to the top of the fence or wall facing the negative feature and grow trailing plants over it. However, trees or the shrubbery should not overshadow or dominate the garden or house. If you have a missing corner in your garden, position a mirror in front of it, just as you would if it featured in the internal structure of the building. Some feng shui practitioners swear by the efficacy of this unusual idea and it creates a novel feature in the garden, as well as making it look bigger by reflecting it back to you.

OBSERVE YOUR CAT

Watch your cat's movement and see where she likes to settle. Obviously, she is going to want to bask in the sun, but if she keeps choosing to stretch out in an area which is shady or damp, perhaps she has located an area of geopathic stress. Alternatively, she may have identified an area of your life which requires the use of some specific feng shui remedies to enhance it.

trees

A garden isn't really a garden without trees, and it's a very unnatural cat that doesn't like to climb them! They provide a great vantage point from which she can survey her territory. I well remember watching my young cat, on one of her first sorties into the great outdoors after all her inoculations, getting tree-climbing lessons from the local ginger tom. While she meowed pitifully underneath, he proceeded to clamber up and down the trunk a few times to show her how it was done. Since she plucked up courage to try it for herself, trees—or the neighbor's greenhouse roof!—have always been one of her favorite refuges, especially as she knows that she can only be retrieved from them with great difficulty, and at risk to life and limb, by her irate owner!

Added to which, of course, cats love to sharpen their claws on wood. They will not do any harm to mature trees this way, although saplings should be protected with wire mesh. It certainly proves less expensive than when they use the furniture in the house!

As wood creatures, cats are naturally going to be drawn to trees and trees are also a very potent force in feng shui. Allow trees to grow naturally and be careful not to change their shape by overzealous pruning. Almost any kind of tree can be of benefit to healthy chi. Fruit trees produce fragrant blossom, while evergreens symbolize long life, although the latter should not be allowed to grow too densely since this can generate harmful chi.

WEEPING WILLOWS

There is some controversy about the role of weeping willows in feng shui. Some practitioners believe that the combined connotation of the name and the fact that their branches droop toward the ground is bad feng shui. Others are content that their beauty and movement make them good feng shui trees and their branches are excellent conductors of chi. This may be a subject on which you have to reach your own conclusion, in conjunction with watching your cat's reaction to the tree! But don't forget that because the tree features strongly on the famous willow pattern plate, they do give your garden a strong flavor of ancient China.

Old trees should never be removed, unless they are dead or dying. Their chi is extremely powerful and feng shui experts believe that they act as acupuncture needles, relieving the pressure which accumulates in the earth. They have been rooted to their spot for far longer than you have been living in your house, so respect their age and the important position they fill, and leave them alone. Sarah Shurety suggests that if you really cannot stand the sight of a tree in your garden, you can improve its appearance by encouraging a creeper to grow round it or by draping it in Christmas tree lights.

ABOVE **Wood is the cat's element, and is better alive than dead. Trees will attract any cat into a garden.**

FAR LEFT **Cats feel at home in trees; they make good observation points**

BELOW **Trees should be respected for their age and their powerful chi.**

plants

According to feng shui precepts, every variety of plant has its own symbolism and, consequently, a particularly auspicious place in which it should be planted within your garden. Both Philippa Waring and Lillian Too have written excellent books on feng shui and gardening (*see Further Reading, p. 157*), in which they list plants which the ancient Chinese considered to be particularly propitious.

FAR RIGHT **Keeping things as natural as possible is good feng shui practice. Obviously, what is natural in China may not be natural elsewhere in the world, but it is better to allow native plants to grow and express their energy than to import exotic plants that may find it difficult to thrive.**

It sounds obvious, but bear in mind the natural growing conditions that your garden offers before deciding what to plant in it and then choose the appropriate plants accordingly. Is the ground well-drained or marshy? The soil acidic or alkaline? Remember that good feng shui practice in the garden involves keeping it as natural as possible and—apart from the amount of effort you will have to expend in trying to keep unsuitable plants alive—a garden containing sickly shrubs that are struggling to survive will not generate healthy chi.

PROPITIOUS PLANTS

Peonies, especially red ones, are thought to bring luck in finding love, particularly for women, but Too points out that if these are hard to obtain, hibiscus and begonias are good substitutes. Chrysanthemums represent long life and so it is a good idea to plant these in your family enrichment area. Fuchsias are considered to be lucky plants and are associated with the fire element, so they should be planted in the south for maximum effect.

However, if your cat repeatedly digs up a plant, it could be a sign that you are overloading a particular enrichment area with a cure which is either too powerful or inappropriate. Try moving it to another location in the garden or removing it altogether.

As you have read earlier, according to feng shui theory, it is extremely unfavorable to have spiky-leaved plants such as cacti within the house. However, the garden is a good place for them—in moderation. It is believed that their spines will ward off evil spirits, and they are especially efficacious when planted on either side of the front of the house.

Once again, this is where that note of common sense comes back into feng shui theory: it is considered permissible to encourage plants with thorns, such as climbing roses, to grow over walls and fences, where not only will their beautiful blooms and fragrance disguise ugly brickwork, but their painful presence will also deter possible intruders! If your neighbors don't like cats, the thorns inherent in a rose-covered wall or a hawthorn fence may also discourage your puss from wandering over the boundary into their yard—although, of course, a truly determined cat will find a way!

RIGHT **Spiky plants, not auspicious inside the home, may be put to good use in the front yard, where their aggressive foliage can deter unwanted visitors.**

water features

By this stage you will realize that water is a very potent remedy in feng shui and your garden is the perfect place in which to employ it. Not only will it enrich your life, but there are few things more soothing than relaxing beside a garden pond or fountain or listening to the gentle sound of water splashing. This is the perfect place to sit with your cat in your lap, restoring your energy, while the water enriches the career, wealth, or family area of your life. It will also draw in "useful friends," such as birds and frogs, which should be reflected by attracting helpful people in your everyday life.

FAR LEFT Whichever water feature you have in your garden, your cat will find it fascinating. If your garden, or your purse, cannot sustain a large pool, a water barrel or a modest pond made from an old stone sink will make harmonious water energy.

RIGHT Choose a round shape for your pond; this will encourage animals such as frogs and birds.

FOUNTAINS AND PONDS

The obvious kind of water feature to choose is a garden pond. A circular pool will be more beneficial than a kidney- or irregularly shaped pond and it should be constructed from a natural material, such as wood or stone, not plastic or fiberglass. However, make sure that your pond is not too big for your garden, or it will swamp the chi within it, doing more harm than good. Also ensure that the water contained in it does not become stagnant or fouled by dead leaves, grass cuttings, or other garden refuse, as this will generate very bad chi.

Moving water is considered more auspicious than still water and so you might consider installing a small fountain. It need not be anything grandiose; a small one will bring the remedies of water, movement, sound, and light into your garden, as well as being a source of pleasure to you and of fascination to your cat. To increase the remedy of light, hang crystals where they will reinforce the reflection of the moving water—but once again, remember that the water cure should be handled with respect, so be careful not to overdo it.

If, for some reason, you really don't want to introduce a specific water feature into the garden, a simple garden faucet, hose, or water barrel can be used as a remedy in the water or wood enrichment area. But if you do use a barrel, please remember to keep it covered and out of reach of curious cats and children.

garden pond

You are already aware of the drawbacks of using fish as a remedy within the home when you are a cat owner. It is really more practical to keep them in the garden, where you can effectively take steps to protect them from your cat. If you have the time to take care of them properly, they are likely to repay the effort generously, as experts believe them to be a very strong feng shui cure. Remember to stock your pool with an odd number of fish—nine, if the pond is big enough—and make sure that one of them is black.

ABOVE RIGHT **Site your pond so that the shallower end faces south; your cat's shadow will be cast on the water as she passes, giving fish the signal to take refuge in deeper water.**

FAR RIGHT **A fish's-eye view of a cat in hunting mode. Water has the power to magnify that which is seen through it.**

BELOW **An odd number of fish is auspicious. Eight gold goldfish and one black one is the best configuration.**

In terms of keeping your fish safe from your cat, in her book *Natural Cats* (see *Further Reading, p. 157*), zoologist and conservationist Chris Madsen suggests siting the shallow end of your pond toward the south, ensuring that your cat —or any other would-be predator—cannot avoid casting its shadow across the shallow water, allowing fish, or other animals attracted to the water, such as frogs, time to escape into the safety of the deeper end.

It is also an excellent idea to put a net over your pond. This will not only prevent your cat and other hunters, such as herons, from scooping out fish, but will also make it easier to retrieve leaves and other garden debris that fall into the pond. If organic matter starts to rot in the pond, it will foul the water and poison your fish, which will induce very bad feng shui.

SAFETY

As with all water features, make sure you take every conceivable step to ensure that it is safe for both your cat and any children. Remember that a child can drown in just a few inches of water and that while cats are interested in water—you only have to observe how intrigued they are by running faucets to realize that—they are by no means good swimmers.

When you construct your pond, make sure that it has a shallow end, or at least ensure that its sides or surrounds slope gradually, rather than shelving deeply. Then, if your cat does forget herself and overreaches while trying to catch a dragonfly, she can climb out with only her dignity given a good soaking. Once again, a net over the pond is a good idea, so she has some leverage if she does fall in.

wildlife

It is very good feng shui to encourage wildlife to frequent your garden. Not only does their activity within your garden stir up chi, but they also bring additional benefits as cures; for example, birdsong is a sound remedy, while the bright hues of butterflies constitute a color cure. Even mice, generally considered to be a pest in the Western world, have a good feng shui influence; they symbolize wealth, because they always locate and amass plentiful food supplies.

However, when you encourage wildlife to frequent your cat's garden, you must obviously at the same time take precautions to protect it. Your cat is a hunter by nature and there is no way that you can stop her from following her instincts. You will no doubt have witnessed her pride in bringing her kill indoors as a trophy for you—and her hurt when you don't always demonstrate suitable appreciation. Ask a friend of mine who was woken at six o'clock one morning by two overexcited, squeaking cats leaping around her bedroom, while the live pigeon one of them had just brought in flapped frantically against the window!

| HUNT SABOTEUR

Cultivating a garden which doubles as a virtual killing-ground is obviously bad feng shui, so offer wildlife as much protection as you can. Attach a bell to your cat's collar; although, in truth, by the time it rings, it will probably be too late for the intended victim. Reflective collars can also help to attract birds' attention to your cat's presence and startle them before she gets a chance to strike. Incidentally, most birds are caught by cats during the twilight hours, so try to keep her indoors at this time.

What may be most effective of all in preventing your cat from catching birds and mammals is a new kind of sonic collar, which has recently come on the market. This senses her muscle movement when she is about to pounce and emits a sound which frightens off prey just as she starts to move. Friends who have used one on their young hunting tomcat report that the tally of trophies that he has brought into the house has been substantially reduced since he has been wearing it.

If you do install a bird feeder or bath to attract birds, make sure that it is placed in the open, well away from overhanging trees, adjoining fences or shed roofs from which your cat could launch herself. Bird houses are probably a bad idea—even if they are placed well out of reach, fledglings usually manage to fall out of them at least once while learning to fly, so unless you're absolutely sure they will be safe from your cat, avoid them.

things to avoid

Aside from cramming your garden full of plants, trees, and ornamental features, there are a number of other things to avoid in planning a feng shui garden to ensure that both you and your cat are able to enjoy spending time in it.

RIGHT **A patch of dense planting will provide a mini jungle for your cat as well as a way of hiding any unsightly objects in the garden.**

Perhaps one of the most important things to remember is that, because you want your garden to be as natural as possible, poisons such as slug pellets, rodent killers, insecticides, pesticides, and lawn spray should not be used. They not only kill pests, but are also potentially lethal for your cat—and also birds and fish—so try to find alternative methods of pest control. Books on organic gardening can give you plenty of tips on how to keep insect numbers down by natural methods, without causing widespread and indiscriminate slaughter.

You should also consider the question of what constitutes a pest in a feng shui garden. Birds will be attracted to a garden where there is a plentiful food supply in the form of slugs, snails, and pesky caterpillars which eventually turn into beautiful butterflies. It may be worth sacrificing a few plants to take advantage of the benefits that accrue when you turn your garden into a haven for wildlife.

BELOW **Some plants can be harmful for your cat, so be aware when you are choosing what to plant or, if you are inheriting a garden, what to uproot.**

On the subject of poisons, be aware that there are certain outdoor plants which can prove harmful to your cat: for example, lupins, sweet peas, holly, clematis, rhododendrons, azaleas, delphiniums, bluebells, and yew. If there is a lawn to distract them, cats will rarely think of chewing garden plants, but in view of the dangers it is probably best to ban potentially harmful plants from your cat's garden.

APPLY YOUR KNOWLEDGE

On a more general level, remember to apply in the garden all the basic feng shui rules that you would use within your home. Keep lawns and paths regularly swept and clear of dead leaves and litter. Make sure that climbing plants are kept pruned and do not allow them to overrun the outside of your house, because in doing so, they are "choking" it, bringing bad health to its occupants. Don't allow weeds to get out of control among the plants in your flowerbeds, but if, on the other hand, you have a lawn, allow daisies and buttercups to flourish there, always remembering you want to keep your garden looking as natural as possible.

Unsightly, but necessary, functional items, such as garbage cans and compost heaps, should be hidden from view. They can be disguised by growing climbing plants on carefully placed trellises or planting dense shrubbery in front of them. Bamboo, which grows very thickly, makes an excellent screen. It also symbolizes good health and longevity for those who live in the house, and the way that it moves and rustles in response to the slightest breeze helps chi to circulate. Your cat will also have hours of fun, stalking around inside it!

small gardens

We can't all be lucky enough to live in a house with a large yard, but we can make the most of the opportunities our home affords. Even a window box is good feng shui, especially if it is located in the southeast. If you don't have enough space for a window box, think about constructing an indoor garden. The simplest way to do this is to attach some trellis to your apartment wall and hang potted plants from it. Indoor gardens are becoming increasingly fashionable and you can find a number of books on the market full of ingenious ideas on this subject.

If you have a paved backyard, you may need to use a bit more imagination, but you'd be surprised at the way in which you can transform it into a little outdoor haven for you and your cat. Some backyards are covered over by ugly, cracked concrete. If you are not allowed, or do not wish, to dig it up, you can cover it in gravel. With the help of a rake, you can create swirling patterns in it; the curves will encourage healthy chi to circulate. Gravel also has the added advantage that you will be able to hear any uninvited intruders in the backyard.

However, do remember that cats dislike the feel of gravel under their feet, so get some circular paving stones and place them over it to make a curving path to a garden bench placed on stone slabs, to which you can retire to relax with a cup of tea, a good book, and your cat in fine weather.

In the absence of flowerbeds, you can plant in wooden tubs or ceramic urns, which are easy to replant and move around when you want to rearrange your garden. Arrange them carefully, placing the tallest plants at the back and the smallest at the front, to give an impression of lush foliage.

▌ ADDITIONAL FEATURES

As you would with a large garden, build yourself a rock garden or cultivate an herb garden in pots. Herbs won't take up much room and the scented varieties such as camomile and thyme will make your garden more fragrant, especially if you live in a city. And there is nothing to beat nipping outside to cut your own chives or basil, or any other herb that you want to add to a recipe! Remember to add some valerian and catnip for your cat as well.

There may even be room for a water feature. You may not have enough space for a pond, but with the increasing popularity of feng shui, manufactured water features can be purchased quite inexpensively. With a bit if ingenuity and know-how, and possibly a pump, you may even be able to make your own from an old wooden half-barrel or from a stack of bowls, arranged so that the water runs from one to the other. This will prove to be a source of endless fascination to your cat and of delightful relaxation for you!

ABOVE **A small garden will look good covered in gravel which can then be raked into auspicious patterns. Provide stepping stones for your cat, who will probably dislike walking on gravel.**

FAR LEFT **Even the narrowest of front yards can be made into an auspicious space with a judicious use of furniture and plants in tubs or pots.**

front gardens

As you read earlier, you should overlay the pa kua on a plan of the front, as well as the back, garden when you are mapping out your enrichment areas out of doors. However, it is probably best not to use your cat as a remedy in the front garden, but encourage her to spend as much time as possible in the back. If you turn this into a real sanctuary for you and your cat, hopefully she won't need too much persuading to spend her time there. It has been said before, but there really is no way to teach your cat road sense, so if she's encouraged to frequent the back garden, rather than the front, there will be less temptation for her to run out into the street.

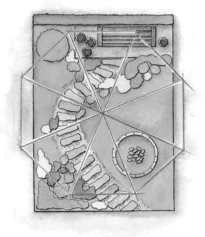

BELOW Traditionally, a pair of urns flanking the front door or gate will provide protection for your house. They need not be as grand as those shown; choose urns or stone figures that suit the style of your house.

Unless you are directly facing a source of bad chi, don't plant high hedges or walls around your front garden to try to keep her in. (It would have to be a very high wall indeed that would stop your cat if she was absolutely determined to explore the road!) A high boundary fence will also prevent chi from entering the property, so use a low wall or fence to represent the phoenix.

If you live in the city and your front yard is only a small, paved area, consider covering it in gravel. Because your cat won't like walking on it, it may deter her from hanging around the

ABOVE Use your pa kua to work out the orientation of your garden and where your enrichment areas fall.

RIGHT Front gardens can be dangerous for cats, who may take the opportunity to run into the street.

front of the house. You can still plant flowers in tubs and pots, which you can move around to change the design of your garden at will.

YOUR FRONT DOOR

In ancient China, main entrances to important buildings were traditionally protected by a pair of "fu dogs," placed on either side of the door. In reality, they were not actually dogs at all, but lions, which used their occult powers to prevent evil spirits and wrongdoers from entering the building. If you can find a pair of fu dogs this would be very auspicious, but if not, Western animals such as griffins or greyhounds would do. Even a pair of urns placed on either side of the door to represent protection would be effective. And you could, of course, always try a pair of stone cats, in place of their bigger, fiercer cousins! Make sure that the area immediately beyond your front door is kept clear, even of beneficial feng shui cures like plants and trees, which will stop chi from entering your home. Sowing grass seed here will attract healthy chi and a bright light will help to draw it into the home.

a feng shui front garden

In this garden, the low wall in the south represents the phoenix, while the shrubs on either side of the house symbolize the tiger and the dragon. Note how the bushes on the dragon's side of the house are kept higher than those on the tiger's side; this helps to keep the latter in check.

RIGHT **A classic feng shui solution to an ordinary front garden. Note the protective twin tubs, the curved path to encourage the flow of chi, the front wall, and the shrubs placed in order to represent the dragon and the tiger.**

BELOW **Young cats should be kept out of the front garden until they develop some road sense.**

The rock garden at the front also represents the phoenix. The gate contains circular patterns to encourage chi and these are echoed in the circular tiles which comprise the path, which is wider at its gate end than at the house, to encourage chi to flow toward the house. A pair of plants in large ceramic pots are placed one on either side of the front door to guard it. Plants such as hydrangeas or roses would be a good choice for the flowerbeds, to entice visitors toward the house, but the roses should be of a variety that doesn't have thorns, since these will indicate harmful intentions toward those who walk up the path. Whatever flowers are used, they should harmonize with the color of the house and with each other, and no more than three different colors should be used; harmonious colours will soothe chi before it enters the house. The tree in the east stimulates the family enrichment, without blocking the flow of chi to the house.

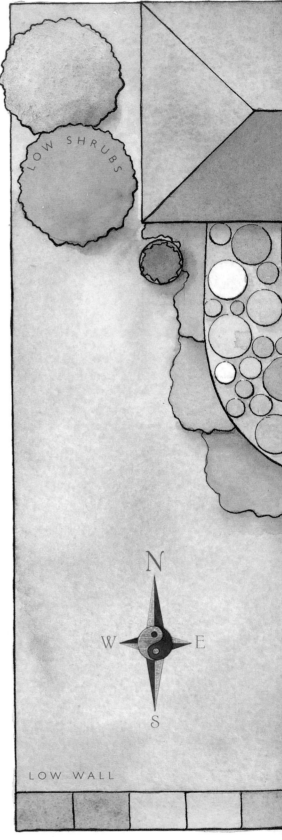

LOW SHRUBS

N
W · E
S

LOW WALL

HOUSE

TALL SHRUBS

TREE

PATH

FLOWERBEDS

ROCK GARDEN

GATE

WALL AND TRELLIS

SUNDIAL

N

W E

S

FLOWERBEDS

STEPPING STONES

FRUIT TREES IN POTS

OUTDOOR CANDLES

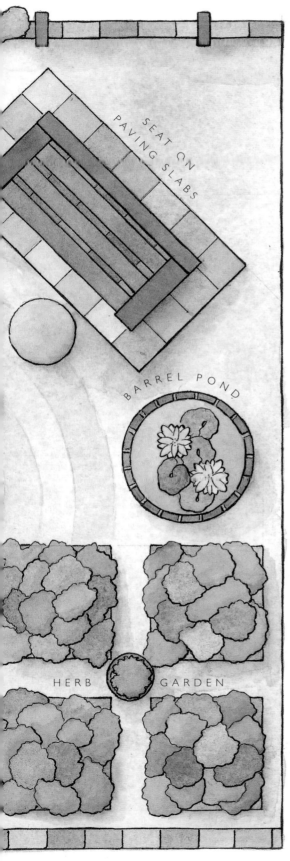

a feng shui small garden

In this backyard garden, the rear wall has been raised with a trellis to represent the tortoise; this helps to support the home, and climbing roses have been cultivated over the rear wall to hide the ugly brickwork, increase privacy, and offer some protection against intruders.

ABOVE Plants can be useful for obscuring brickwork or shielding private areas.

The whole area has been covered in colored gravel, arranged in swirling patterns to increase the flow of chi, while circular paving stones (for the cat's convenience!) lead in a meandering path to the garden seat. Placed in the north-east, this offers a relaxing view of the plants against the west wall, and because it is placed in the education area, it will be a good place to sit and read. The plants in the west have been ranged in height order to give the impression of lush vegetation, while the half-barrel water feature increases relaxation with the sound of gently splashing water. A pair of small fruit trees, planted in ceramic pots, stands in the southwest corner to encourage a fruitful relationship, and an herb garden is within easy reach of the kitchen door. A pair of large barbecue candles brings extra illumination to the fame enrichment locality, and a sundial enhances the helpful people area. The whole garden has been designed to allow the free flow of chi energy.

LEFT A feng shui solution for a small garden using gravel instead of grass and strategic enhancements in each enrichment area.

a feng shui garden for children

In this garden the children's toys are placed on the west side of the garden, which is their enrichment area. The metal of the slide in the northwest corner is also an enhancement of the helpful people area.

The sandpit enhances the relationships corner, governed by the earth element, while the paddling pool introduces water to wealth enrichment. The wooden table and chairs are somewhere where the whole family can sit together in their own sheltered enrichment area, but if any of the children want to study out of doors, they can easily be moved along into the shadier education corner. The barbecue in the south is conveniently close to the house and brings welcome fire to the fame enrichment area. The tortoise sculpture (although a live one would do just as well) represents the Form School tortoise, supporting the household, while the bird table is isolated in the middle of the lawn where its occupants will be able to see a predatory cat coming!

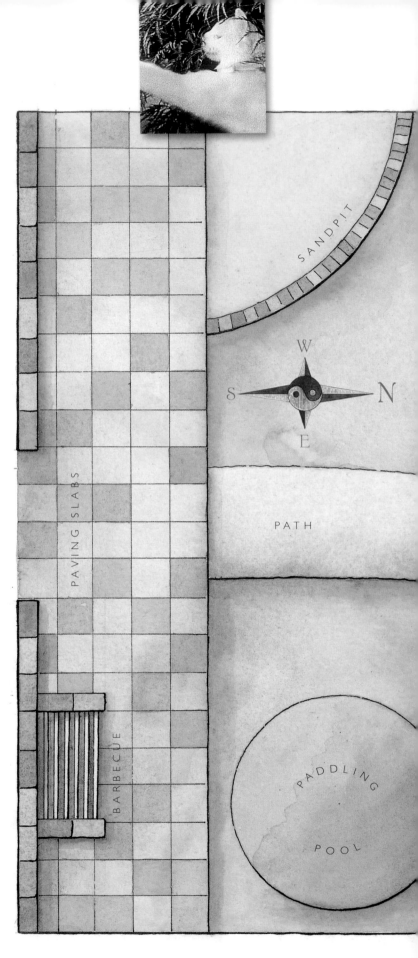

SANDPIT

W N S E

PATH

PAVING SLABS

BARBECUE

PADDLING POOL

RIGHT **A garden which unites the needs of children with suitable placement of enhancements in each enrichment area.**

SLIDE

SWING

TORTOISE
SCULPTURE

BIRD
FEEDER

TABLE
AND CHAIRS

TRELLIS

TREES

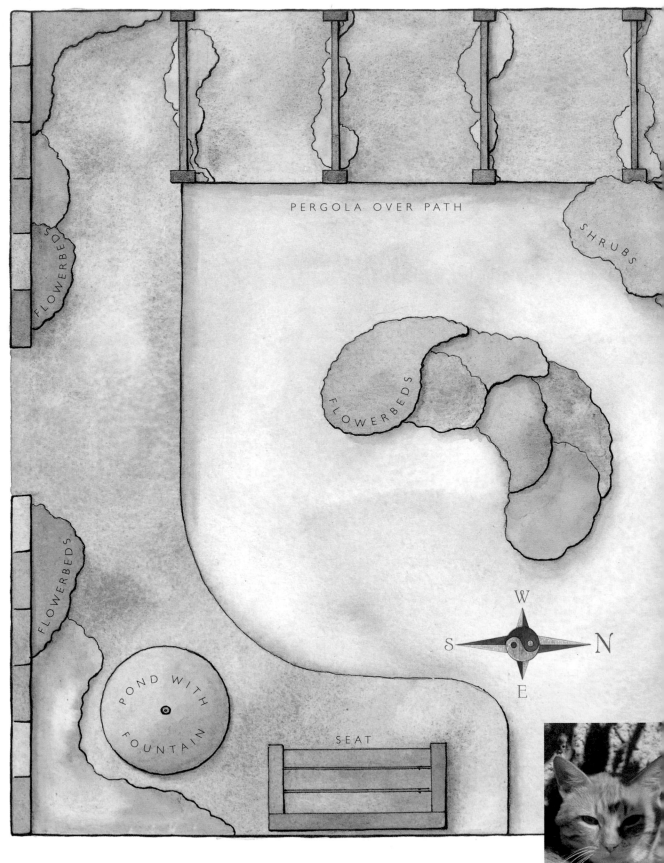

PERGOLA OVER PATH

SHRUBS

FLOWERBEDS

FLOWERBEDS

FLOWERBEDS

W

S ⊕ N

E

POND WITH FOUNTAIN

SEAT

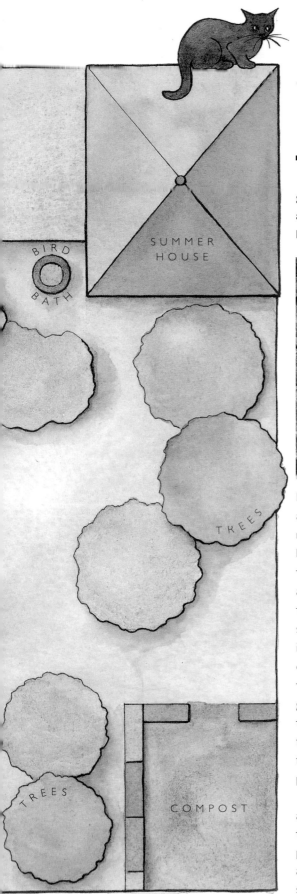

a feng shui restful garden

This is a garden aimed at rest and relaxation. The rather harsh, straight line of the path on the western side of the garden is softened by the arching pergola covered in flowers, and it leads visitors up to the secret summer house, largely hidden by the bushes in front of it.

LEFT Don't position trees near a bird bath, or your cat will have a field day.

In the summer house, people can sit in privacy and watch the birds visiting the bird bath—but make sure that it is well out of reach of the bushes and trees, so that your cat cannot use them for camouflage! A compost heap may appear to be inauspicious, but it is a useful thing to have in a garden. Place it in the education sector, because it is something which is maturing, and wall it in, so it can't be seen. The occupants of the house can also sit in the relationship area, and appreciate the beauty of the garden and its pond and fountain, which are in the wealth corner. A few red flowers in the flowerbeds in the south would enhance the fame area here, and red flowers, particularly peonies, can help with relationships as well.

This is a good garden for cats, with its trees and summer house designed for climbing practice. Don't forget, however, that ponds are a potential hazard, and some netting stretched across will protect your cat—as well as shielding the fish from predatory paws!

LEFT A garden designed using feng shui principles to promote privacy, peace, and serene relaxation.

a Chinese-style feng shui garden

This garden is strongly influenced by traditional Chinese gardens—think of the willow tree pattern plate! Most of the flowers you plant in this garden should be white, with just the occasional flash of color to provide contrast.

The winding path leads through the trees to a pagoda-style summer house, looking out over the pond, which is crossed by a decorative Chinese bridge. In the northeast is a traditional Chinese rock garden, hidden behind a wall covered in trailing plants. The bamboo hedge symbolizes the tortoise and creates an attractive boundary for the rear of the garden. There is a pair of ornamental heron statues in the relationship area, signifying good luck in love, while the wind chime in the southeast stimulates the wealth area. Lights in the south symbolize fire to enhance the fame area. The garden seat is enclosed by trellises covered with flowers, creating an area for meditation, and it looks out over a bed of plants, symbolizing the family.

RIGHT For purists, a garden designed in the Chinese style, complete with herons and a decorative bridge.

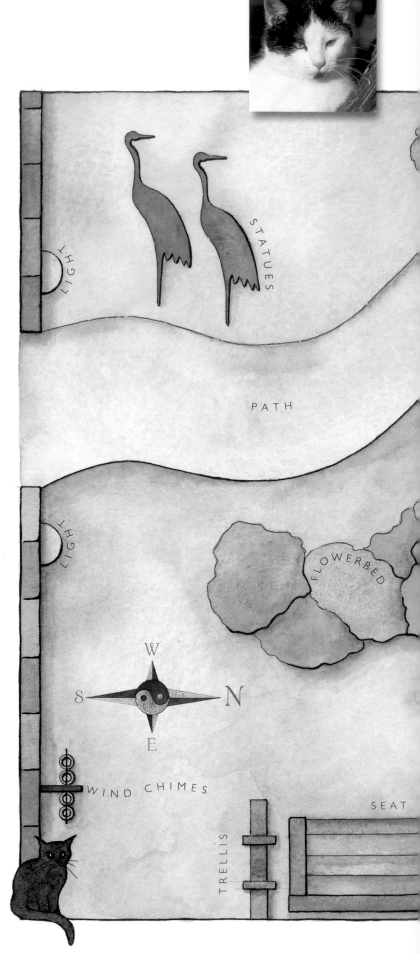

152

FLOWERBED

TREE

FLOWERBED

TREE

SUMMER HOUSE

BAMBOO HEDGE

POND

BRIDGE

WALL

ROCK GARDEN

afterword

By now, you will have become more familiar with the ways in which sensitively working with your cat, in conjunction with employing the basic principles of feng shui, can help you to improve the environment in which you live and, consequently, a variety of different areas within your life.

The most important thing to bear in mind when following the recommendations in this book is not to take them too literally, or seriously. Different remedies can be expected to work in different ways for different people, so keep experimenting and adjusting until you find the most effective remedies for you—and bear in mind that their efficacy will probably fade after a while, so that you may then need to try something new.

Don't try to force your cat into behavior that is unnatural for her. Remember that she has an innate sensitivity as to what is required to adjust levels of energy within the home to healthy levels, and her intuition should be respected—unless, of course, her actions cause too much inconvenience within your house or are injurious to her health. Do bear in mind at all times that the happier your cat is, the better the feng shui will be inside your home. Take care of her and in return, she will take care of you.

Have fun with your feng shui experiments; it is a fascinating art and once you have become well-versed in the basic principles, you may find that you want to learn more about it and study it in greater depth. And even if you don't believe that it can help to bring major changes to your life, you will at least find that by following its precepts, you will have a cleaner, neater, and more attractive-looking home—which will, of course, give you an improved quality of life in itself! So, along with a bit of help from your cat, why not try to improve your life with feng shui? All you have to lose is your clutter!

glossary

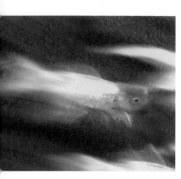

celestial animals—the four animals inherent in Form School feng shui.

chakras—the seven areas within the body where chi is most concentrated.

chi—the electromagnetic force which flows throughout the universe.

Compass School—a school of feng shui which identifies and enhances enrichment areas through the use of the pa kua.

destructive cycle—the cycle in which the five elements destroy each other.

earth luck—luck generated by surrounding circumstances.

enrichment area—one of the eight fundamental areas in life.

feng shui—literally, "wind and water." The ancient Chinese art of harmonizing the environment to create the best circumstances in which luck can operate.

five elements—the principal energies of the universe.

Form School—The oldest school of feng shui, concerned with the effect external environmental factors have on the home.

geopathic stress—natural earth radiation which has been distorted, thus making it potentially harmful.

heaven luck—luck dictated by the heavens (roughly, the Eastern equivalent of the Western concept of fate).

humankind luck—luck created by human endeavor.

missing corner—missing enrichment area.

pa kua—octagonal compass used to identify the enrichment areas.

poison arrow—a sharp angle or straight line which concentrates chi dangerously at its point.

productive cycle—the cycle in which the five elements nurture each other.

remedy—a means of enhancing an enrichment area.

sha chi—dangerous, fast-running chi.

sheng chi—perfectly balanced chi.

si chi—harmful, slow-moving chi.

space clearing—a technique for cleansing and/or dispersing bad energy.

tao—the combination of yin and yang which unites humans with the universe.

Taoism—ancient Chinese religion.

yang—pertaining to the realm of the ethereal. The opposite of yin.

yin—pertaining to the realm of the earthly. The opposite of yang.

FURTHER READING

BASIC FENG SHUI: AN ILLUSTRATED REFERENCE MANUAL, Lillian Too, Oriental Publications, 1997

CHINESE ANIMAL SYMBOLISMS, Ong Hean-Tatt, Pelanduk Publications, 1997

THE COMPLETE ILLUSTRATED GUIDE TO FENG SHUI FOR GARDENS, Lillian Too, Element, 1998

CREATING SACRED SPACE WITH FENG SHUI, Karen Kingston, Broadway Books, 1998

GARDEN FENG SHUI: A BEGINNER'S GUIDE, Roni Jay, Hodder & Stoughton, 1999

FENG SHUI FOR BEGINNERS, Richard Craze, Trafalgar Square, 1999

FENG SHUI FOR BEGINNERS, Richard Webster, Llewellyn Publications, 1997

FENG SHUI FOR YOUR HOME, Sarah Shurety, Trafalgar Square, 1997

THE FENG SHUI GARDEN, Gill Hale, Storey Books, 1998

THE FENG SHUI OF GARDENING, Philippa Waring, Souvenir Press, 1998

THE FENG SHUI HOUSE BOOK, Gina Lazenby, Watson-Guptill Publications, 1998

INTERIOR DESIGN WITH FENG SHUI, Sarah Rossbach, E.P. Dutton, 1997

THE MAGICAL LORE OF CATS, Marion Davies, Capall Bann Publishing, 1998

NATURAL CATS, Chris Madsen, Howell Book House, 1997

PRINCIPLES OF FENG SHUI, Simon Brown, Thorsons, 1996

ASPCA COMPLETE CAT CARE MANUAL, Andrew Edney, DK Publishing, 1992

SACRED SPACE, Denise Linn, Ballantine Books, 1995

SIMPLY FENG SHUI FOR HOME, OFFICE & GARDEN, Wendy Hobson, Foulsham, 1998

index

PICTURE CREDITS

Art Directors & Trip A. Cowin 108 / E. R. Doubleday 72 / H. Gariety 143 / S. Grant 23, 31 / G. Harris 54 / R. Langfield 26, 52, 80, 96 / Helene Rogers 147 / V. Schwanberg 20 / J. Stanley 24, 76 / Streano/Havens 12 / Viesti Collection 14/15, 42/43, 100/101, 126/127, 144; **Bruce Coleman Collection** Adriano Bacchella 39, 46L, 119 / Jane Burton 2, 48, 49, 63, 67, 94/95, 104, 106, 115, 116/117, 128, 131, 151, 154/155 / Bruce Coleman Inc. 62B / Werner Layer 81T, 120 / Robert Maier 74/75, 99 / Hans Reinhard 36, 46/47, 55, 71, 79, 83, 87, 110/111, 121, 123, 129 / Kim Taylor 132/133; **ET Archive** British Library 9/ Musée du Louvre, Paris 13B; **Garden Picture Library** Jerry Pavia 118; **Hulton Getty** 30T; **The Image Bank** Rob Atkins 60 / P. E. Berglund 28 / Steve Bronstein 102B / Bullaty/Lomeo 16, 140 / G. K. & Vikki Hart 92, 135 / John P. Kelly 19 / Carol Kohen 27 / David de Lossy 40 / Ira Montgomery 73 / Marti Pie 8 / Malcolm Piers 32 / P. Proehl 56 / Terje Rakke 7 / Antonio Rossario 136 / Nicholas Russell 57, 70 / Dag Sundberg 84; **The Stockmarket** C. B. Productions 51 / Koopman 6 / Don Mason 64 / Roy Morsch 68 / Jose Fuste Raga 93 / Rob & Sas 45 / John M. Roberts 139; **Tony Stone Images** Glen Allison 17B / Jim Corwin 10/11 / Bruno Dittrich 124/125 / David Glick 77T / Darrell Gulin 44 / Roy Gumpel 105 / Claire Hayden 101T, 136 / Walter Hodges 34/35, 112/113 / Rich Iwasaki 29 / Kathi Lamm 88, 102/103T / Renée Lynn 110L / Roine Magnusson 93 / Thomas Peterson 58/59 / Paul Redman 69 / Leslie Sponseller 33T / Frank Siteman 90/91 / Robert Stahl 106/107 / Terry Vine 97 / Paul Wakefield 82. Every effort has been made to trace all copyright holders and obtain permissions. The editors and publishers sincerely apologize for any inadvertent errors or omissions, and will be happy to correct them in any future editions.

ACKNOWLEDGMENTS

The publishers would like to thank the following for providing props for photography: **The Feng Shui Company** (for mail order telephone/fax (+44) 7000 781901); **The Geomancer** (for consultation and courses, telephone (+44) 7000 888989; for mail order telephone (+44)1483 839898); **Curiouser and Curiouser**, Brighton, England; **Evolution**, Brighton, England; **The Animal House**, Brighton, England; **Wilkinson's,** Brighton, England; **Earthly Artefacts**, Brighton, England; **Angelic,** Brighton, England; **Winfalcon's Healing Centre**, Brighton, England; **Botanica**, Brighton, England; **Adaptatrap**, Brighton, England; **Daryl Macke**, Brighton, England; **Elephant**, Brighton and stores around the UK; **Heavenly Realms**, Brighton, England; **Roost**, Brighton, England; **Alan Stirling** at the **Feng Shui Workshop**, telephone (+44)1634 300887; **Amanda Gearing**, feng shui consultant, telephone (+44)1273 478108. Thanks also to **Frankie Goldstone**, and to **Florence** and **Tweaker** for inspiration.